CH00866647

Unwin Education Books

WORLD FAITHS IN EDUCATION

Unwin Education Books

Series Editor: Ivor Morrish, BD, BA, Dip.Ed. (London), BA (Bristol)

Education Since 1800 IVOR MORRISH
Moral Development WILLIAM KAY
Physical Education for Teaching BARBARA CHURCHER
The Background of Immigrant Children IVOR MORRISH
Organising and Integrating the Infant Day JOY TAYLOR
The Philosophy of Education: An Introduction HARRY SCHOFIELD
Assessment and Testing: An Introduction HARRY SCHOFIELD
Education: Its Nature and Purpose M. V. C. JEFFREYS
Learning in the Primary School KENNETH HASLAM
The Sociology of Education: An Introduction IVOR MORRISH
Developing a Curriculum AUDREY and HOWARD NICHOLLS
Teacher Education and Cultural Change H. DUDLEY PLUNKETT and
    JAMES LYNCH
Reading and Writing in the First School JOY TAYLOR
Approaches to Drama DAVID A. MALE
Aspects of Learning BRIAN O'CONNELL
Focus on Meaning JOAN TOUGH
Moral Education WILLIAM KAY
Concepts in Primary Education JOHN E. SADLER
Moral Philosophy for Education ROBIN BARROW
Beyond Control? PAUL FRANCIS
Principles of Classroom Learning and Perception RICHARD J. MUELLER
Education and the Community ERIC MIDWINTER
Creative Teaching AUDREY and HOWARD NICHOLLS
The Preachers of Culture MARGARET MATHIESON
Mental Handicap: An Introduction DAVID EDEN
Aspects of Educational Change IVOR MORRISH
Beyond Initial Reading JOHN POTTS
The Foundations of Maths in the Infant School JOY TAYLOR
Common Sense and the Curriculum ROBIN BARROW
The Second 'R' WILLIAM HARPIN
The Diploma Disease RONALD DORE
The Development of Meaning JOAN TOUGH
The Countesthorpe Experience JOHN WATTS
The Place of Commonsense in Educational Thought LIONEL ELVIN
Language in Teaching and Learning HAZEL FRANCIS
Patterns of Education in the British Isles NIGEL GRANT and
    ROBERT BELL
Philosophical Foundations for the Curriculum ALLEN BRENT
World Faiths in Education W. OWEN COLE
Classroom Language: What Sort? JILL RICHARDS

Contents

PART THREE

This book is written in the hope that religious education will continue to develop in such a way that all who are committed to the importance of life may feel able to bring their insights to bear upon it so that its worthwhileness may be enhanced in a subject which is both dynamic and truly professional.

It is respectfully dedicated to friends and colleagues of many faiths from whom I have learned much and to the students of James Graham College, Leeds, from whom I gained far more than I have given.

Many people have been involved in the preparation of this book and acknowledgement is due to them all. I especially wish to thank the copy editors for their patient help.

Introduction

The world religions movement, as it is sometimes called, is one major influence upon the curriculum development of religious education today. The name is unfortunate. It suggests that battle lines are drawn up with Christianity or evangelism on one side and the world religions on the other. It also implies that those who have contributed to the changes which have resulted in Islam or Judaism being taught in our schools have merely been content to append these to existing structures. Neither allegation is true. The eagerness to have Christianity fairly and comprehensively presented is no less than the concern for Islam, and most of those active in world religions are also engaged in the total re-appraisal of religious education which is now taking place. The essays which form this book are an attempt to put world religions in their total school context. Hopefully, they also share insights and deeper understandings acquired as a result of experience and reflection upon it. A few years ago, in 1970 or thereabouts, teachers began to scramble for places on the world religions bandwagon, and some courses were introduced without much thought being given to the consequences. Now we are older, if not wiser, and whilst continuing the journey we can give some attention to issues which have arisen along the way. Two are of burning urgency—those of commitment and the teaching of Christianity. Others are becoming increasingly important—the teaching of Humanism and Marxism. Even more significant in the long term is the change which has enabled some Jews, Muslims and Humanists, though not all, to feel that they have a contribution to make not only in providing materials and writing about the subject, but also by serving on Agreed Syllabus Conferences and, most important, teaching it in the classroom.

Let us consider these issues for a moment, noting that they will arise again, at various places, in the chapters which follow.

Commitment is of prime value and importance to a religious person and also to a Humanist or Marxist. All these faiths have their martyrs for the truth as they have perceived it. To exclude commitment from the classroom would seem to be an act of emasculation. However, in education there are appropriate and inappropriate ways of expressing and examining it. If the word 'honesty' is used instead, we may have gone some distance towards discovering ways which are proper—for honesty demands that we declare our stance, honesty requires that we recognise that it is not universally accepted, and honesty prevents us trying to press-gang children into the kingdom of God or the republic of Marx by using methods of misrepresentation or deceit. Honesty must extend to making schools places where children learn about life, including religion, sex, morality, politics and government, but free from the pressures of propaganda.

In this ideal setting, or even in the real secular society in which we live, Christianity can no longer be taught as it used to be. The basic assumption that it is true is one which society no longer holds. The presentation of Judaism or Islam as a rounded whole requires Christianity to be taught in a similar way, or 16-year-olds may leave school with a sound knowledge of the beliefs and practices of Islam as a living faith and an awareness of Christianity as no more than Bible-related neighbourliness and decency!

Teachers seem to be prepared to concede a place for Humanism but not for Marxism. The Humanist question seems to be confined to attitudes and materials, the open recognition that there are those who accept a naturalistic interpretation of human existence and the need for adequate teaching-aids. The latter Humanists must be prepared to provide.

One of the most personally exciting things that has happened to me in the last decade in the area of religious education is the dialogue I have begun with people of many faiths about education in general and religious education in particular. This book could not have been written but for these exchanges in the context of friendship and mutual respect. I welcome Humanists, Muslims and Jews with their very different concerns and outlooks as participants in my profession. But it requires them to learn the rules and not to become the evangelist I have ceased to be, as it requires me to change some rules and more attitudes so that they can become my fellow-workers.

In a pluralistic world there is little to be gained by concealing differences. In school, in ways appropriate to the child's growth and depending upon circumstances, these can be dealt with in a context of security. At the infant stage it may be no more, and no less, than openly accepting Jaswant's long hair and his dad's turban, Pushpa's sari and vegetarianism, or the fact that Alan's family goes to church but Jayne's does not. Later it will involve the recognition that Jews and Muslims do not accept the divinity of Jesus and that most Marxists are atheists, though in parts of South America it may be possible to speak of a Christian Marxist! How far should we go in giving atheism a hearing? In some Communist countries Jews, Christians and Muslims are being persecuted because of their beliefs. Despite this, should children be allowed to learn about Marxist beliefs and practices? Each teacher must decide such matters for himself. I would not like Marxism to be misrepresented by a hostile teacher. However, I would plead for a number of questions to be considered. First, is it proper that Marxism should be left to propagandists and the media when it is such an important influence upon our lives? Secondly, can we dodge responsibility by passing the task to the historian? Who claims to deal in beliefs and ideologies, him or us? If he ignores Islam when he teaches about the Crusades, can we expect him to outline Marxist philosophy in his study of Soviet Russia? What kind of logic allows us to teach about Islam, which denies man's need for a saviour, and Judaism, which rejects Jesus' divinity, but will not countenance the teaching of Marxism? As I have already said, it is for each teacher or each school to provide answers; but, if openness is to mean anything, the question must be raised. This service I hope this book will provide.

As the last chapter indicates, illogicalities persist—they always will. Mankind, his institutions and his activities are never rigidly logical whilst they are human and alive, and I certainly do not wish religion in schools to be anything but warm and vital. So let there be illogicality, but let there also be dialectic. Religious education teachers probably gather together more than most. Whether it be through the work of the Christian Education Movement, Association for Religious Education, the Shap Working Party, Birmingham or Bradford Agreed Syllabus Conferences, the Standing Committee on Inter-faiths Dialogue in Religious Education, or the Association of Christian Teachers, they meet, they discuss, they benefit from an exchange of views. Long may the various bodies continue their work, though in difficult economic times all, being voluntary, are struggling. They bring their various insights to bear upon the common interest—the improved teaching of religious education—and they share in the great debate. Through local education authority advisory services, which over the last few years have increased tremendously in RE, the small hard core of teachers who resist re-education in any area of the curriculum is gradually being reached.

This book itself contains illogicalities, the most glaring being the inclusion of contributions written by people from their particular life-stance (to use Harry Stopes-Roe's term) viewpoints. RE in maintained schools is becoming independent of confessional bodies, I hope, but a consequence of the Christian denominations' readiness to hand responsibility to the university, college and school specialists has been the resulting feeling of other faiths that they can now participate. Eventually the day may be reached when the one label will suffice (but not 'RE specialist', if Humanists are to feel comfortable), just as it does for history or physics, but it has not dawned yet.

Islam, Judaism and Hinduism are well covered elsewhere, and therefore this book has contented itself with issues which result from teaching world faiths in general and Buddhism, Marxism and Humanism in particular. A serious written symposium on the teaching of Buddhism in schools is something which Buddhist specialists must still provide. For the moment Dave Williams has pinpointed some of the major issues as well as can be done within the limits of one chapter and so plugged the gap. For projects, bibliographies, tools for teaching world religions the teacher is referred to the Shap Working Party—Community Relations Commission handbook which I have edited under the title *World Religions: a Handbook for Teachers* (Community Relations Commission, 1977).*

An increasing number of us today are arguing that RE in county schools should be neither faith-creating nor faith-destroying. It should be concerned with knowledge (for example, what a Humanist or Christian believes, or how people worship), with understanding (what it means to be a Muslim or a Jew), and with helping the pupil to become a mature human being. If he finds this maturity in his Muslim, Jewish, Christian or Humanist background, so be it; the teacher is there to help the pupil in his search and not to make him arrive at some predetermined Christian or Marxist destination. My sections in this book are written from that standpoint and in that spirit. I have not tried to dominate my fellow-contributors and I do not seek the agreement of my readers. I simply ask them to share with me a concern for the subject, for all its constituent elements, and for the various commitments of all who are involved, both teachers and children.

*Second edition has been published by Commission for Racial Equality.

PART ONE

An attempt to place the teaching of world religions in its total subject context and to consider some issues which frequently concern teachers of RE, especially of world religions.

Chapter 1

Towards a Total View of Religion in School

Religion in school might be described as an appendix without a body. Once the body was definite, it was the Bible, but in many schools today the Judaeo-Christian scriptures have themselves become an appendix at the end of a life-theme, or an afterthought to Hinduism or one of the other Eastern faiths.

There is no system, no logic, no model. Therefore, at the beginning of a book which intentionally concentrates upon the most recently popular appendix it seems necessary to attempt the daunting task of constructing a total anatomy, so that the appendix, if such it is eventually seen to be, may have its proper location and function.

The natural starting-point is a consideration of aims short term, but more especially long term, so that a philosophy may emerge.

It is easy to produce a list of topics which may keep the 'Rosla' type of pupil fairly quiet and attentive. Often the resulting course will prompt him to be reflective about the meaning of life, especially in terms of personal relations, but it may lack any ultimate goal. It may not examine how people, be they atheist or religious, attempt to work out a coherent approach to life. Such a course would seem to be no more than fragmentary, a series of case-studies only hopefully relevant to living as he is to experience it once school is behind him.

Such an approach can also be no more than a study of human relationships. There is more to life than this. Each human being has also to come to terms with himself. If he is at all reflective, he also needs to work out his relationship with the reality of which he is a part—that which believers of various faiths often call God. An adequate religious education would examine ultimate questions and a variety of answers which are given to them, atheistic and theistic. It would also attempt to probe to the heart of topical and perennial relationship-issues—peace, race, friendship and the like. In addition it would examine personal issues which are manifested in the pop scene, drugs, youth cults, all of which seem to be related to a search for identity, meaning and coherence. It would, however, be the under-lying concern, not only the manifestations, which the teacher would hope to help the pupils explore.

Besides examining the three areas of life which have been mentioned—the self, human relationships, the relationship of this self to life as a whole—the teacher must decide why the study is being made.

Traditionally, in Britain, and still in many areas of the world, education has been a process of induction into society. The beliefs, attitudes and the basic skills which the culture accepts and wishes to preserve are transmitted through the school as well as the home. Education therefore plays an important conservative role. However, education in Britain and other parts of the Western world has, in recent years, changed direction. Gradually, throughout this century, the emphasis has been more upon knowledge and skills, less upon attitudes and induction into the beliefs and behaviour-norms of the culture. Almost by accident we have invited people to exercise independent judgement, to make up their own minds, at the very moment in history when the normal constraints of religion, patriotism, a sense of national unity and purpose have also become weak in their influence. In consequence Muslims especially, coming to Britain from Pakistan, express horror at what they mistakenly describe as the permissiveness of British society. Their real anxiety, because of their strong sense of community and family solidarity, has to do with our alien way of life, which is individualistic. The 'permissive' manifestation is less important than the dangers of exposing children to an educational process and society which invite them to think and act for themselves without necessarily considering the beliefs or advice of the community.

Whether the teacher likes it or not, and whatever opinion polls conducted among parents may say, this attempt to induct children into a system of beliefs and pattern of behaviour is no longer possible in Britain. A swing in the attitude of society at large resulting in an affirmation of the old values might make traditional education once more practicable. However, such change is unlikely and, I would add, unhealthy. Maturity and the compulsion of a public opinion eager to ostracise its non-conformists are incompatible; to hope for its return is unworthy and desperate.

Religion in education can no longer, therefore, imitate the believing community. It cannot stand as a spire, a minaret, a rock pointing the way to salvation whilst the rest of the curriculum, the school staff, and society as a whole state that there are many ways—or perhaps none at all. For this reason, among others, compulsory school worship in maintained schools must disappear. This act of affirmation in God's existence—for worship is surely that—is one of the remaining sad attempts of established belief to retain its position of privilege. It is the sore thumb of the curriculum.

In the curriculum, however, the importance of religious studies is enhanced, once the traditional purpose of inducting pupils into belief has been rejected. It can now play its proper part together with other aspects of the curriculum as an academic discipline. It can also accept its place, which few would reject, in helping to equip young people to face life.

First, let us consider the subject as an academic discipline, using the term 'academic' in the rather specialised context of the school.

Here it will never be the arid imparting of knowledge and information for completely purist academic reasons. The dullness of reading the Bible round the class need not be replaced by an equally boring reading of the Gita or Qur'an as some wish to assume! Related to reality, it will have to do with practices as well as with ideas, with ritual as well as belief. Again, related to reality, it will perforce go beyond but not exclude Christianity, and one hopes it will encourage Christian studies to free itself from an inhibitory and unreal preoccupation with the Bible, to the neglect of music, drama, art and ritual, all of which compound to produce the richness of that religion. Where the course touches on theology one hopes it will do so not abstractly but through stating the problems which theology attempts to solve—the nature of the universe, the forgiveness of sin, the problem of undeserved suffering.

Secondly, whilst it should not be the teacher's aim to produce Christians, he is a member of an institution which regards itself as having a responsibility for producing thoughtful, feeling, perceptive human beings. Alongside all his colleagues the teacher of religious studies is involved in this work. It is not a solo effort to be undertaken in a weekly forty-minute lesson with a single specified goal in mind— the acceptance of a religious view of life. It implies an openness of approach and a variety of content going far beyond leaving the pupil free to accept or reject Christianity; it must apprise him of the existence of other responses to life which are not religious, the atheistic and Marxist. This must be done in a spirit of fairness, repudiating the taking advantage of immature minds by using dishonest arguments.

It will be seen that the work of the religious studies teacher is wide-ranging, serious and challenging. He is concerned with enabling the pupil, by the time he leaves school, to be aware of something of the place and function of religion in human experience. This entails understanding the questions religions ask and the solutions they offer. It involves knowing what it means to be a Christian or a Hindu in terms of practice and belief. It also involves, as part of this exercise, the task of penetrating to the heart of human experience so that the questions may be seen to be real and important. There is then no conflict between implicit and explicit religion when this is appreciated. The two meet together in the exploration of life, and only conflict when the one becomes a mere secular-based exploration of personal relationships permitting no possibility of religious views being correct or worth considering or even knowing, and the other a descriptive naming of the parts. Finally, it requires on the part of pupil and teacher the recognition that this is not religious studies. It is something more. It is the study of life, for it is not—as 'religious studies' implies —an exercise in which only the believer can engage; nor is it one to which the only possible solutions, if the pupil wishes to find them, are religious.

Perhaps at this point one can construct a skeleton upon which comment can then be made.

(1) The Early Years. Experiential teaching related to
myself
myself and others
myself and the cosmos.

(2) The Middle Years. Further experiential teaching related to the above but also a direct exploration into religion through its phenomena.

(3) The Later Years. Further exploration into the phenomena, but accompanied by a move from practices to ideas and beliefs, and ending with ultimate questions about the meaning of life and an examination of the various explanations and interpretations which are possible. In short, this will be a return to the initial areas of concern, but not this time to explore and enrich experience but to consider its meaning.

THE DEVELOPMENT OF THIS OUTLINE

Having in the first section argued my way towards the simple model outlined above, perhaps it is now convenient to attempt to cover the bare bones with flesh.

The Early Years

With the youngest children it would seem that the first requirement is the provision, enrichment and exploration of experience in a total context of security. In general terms, the views of R. S. Lee (*Your Growing Child and Religion*, Penguin, 1965) and Ronald Goldman (*Religious Thinking from Childhood to Adolescence*, Routledge & Kegan Paul, 1964) are accepted. Over-simply stated, I would argue that R. S. Lee suggests that the needs, desires and feelings with which religion has to do are adult in an explicit sense; these are present in children, of course, but the parent or teacher is the person who can satisfy them. God for the young child is an unnecessary postulate. Love, forgiveness, loneliness, suffering are provided or dealt with in the home and school atmosphere. Similarly, following Ronald

Goldman, the cognitive aspects of religion are as incomprehensible to the young child as the affective are unreal. Consequently, religion is not something relevant to the personal interior life of young children outside the environment of a religious home. The early school years should therefore be thought of as pre-religious, and the content of the syllabus should take this into account.

This means that explicit religious material—Bible stories or the use of hymns and prayers—should be minimal or non-existent and the onus should always be upon the teacher to justify them. Not only is the religious material irrelevant to the child and liable to be misunderstood, but its use is also very often stultifying, in that it interprets experience and deflects the child's thinking from those things which are of interest to him to a being who is remote and apparently part of a fantasy world. 'The Lord God made them all' is a conclusion some children may reach. In late-twentieth-century Britain it is not an assumption which we should ask the five-year-old in our state schools, who does not come from a believing home, to accept.

Instead, one might healthily and meaningfully begin with experience. For some children this needs to be provided, for all enrichment and exploration of experience are needed.

A start might be made with *myself*. Who am I? Concentration will be upon the five senses, first becoming aware of them but gradually, too, becoming more appreciative of them; becoming more sensitive to them, if the pun may be pardoned. Of course, science and language also begin at this point in the first or infant school. Has pre-religious education any distinctive contribution to make? Certainly. In the area which we might call 'psychological' especially. In exploring feelings of anger, frustration or failure, or noticing how we possess power as well as skill in our hands, power to do good or speak kind words, power to break, destroy and hurt—as we consider these we are posing the question 'Who am I?' at its most profound level.

As we consider the second area, *myself and others*, we may also probe situations which anticipate the direct examination of the ethical and social dimensions of religion. The Wendy-house experiences, the new types of relationship which almost every child is making in his first months at school, present in a very real form an awareness of envy, greed, kindness, friendship, tolerance and the ability to live with differences. It must be asked what, if anything, would religious stories of Jesus and Zacchaeus, of Muhammad and the Unkind Camel Driver, add to a deep exploration of these experiences? Such stories do have a place in the appropriate circumstances, and this will be discussed elsewhere, but the present argument is that if one is exploring the idea of friendship with young children the 'life' element (some would prefer 'religious' element) lies in the depth of the exploration and not in the use of religious material. The story of David and Jonathan, especially if explored through movement or drama, *might* enrich the study, but the mere telling of the story in itself would do nothing more than provide an unsure teacher with the feeling that the theme had been given a religious dimension. It is doubtful whether this illusion would have been shared by the children.

Myself and the cosmos may sound rather pretentious. The phrase is used to express a desire to refer to more that the scientific, biological relationship which man has with the world around him. Awe and wonder, an awareness of beauty, ugliness and mystery, are ideas as perplexing as man's ascent or descent from the ape. Largely, but not solely, through the observation of nature, and especially of seasonal change, this area of experience may be provided, enriched and explored, but not to the point of saying 'The Lord God made them all,' or 'Darwinian evolutionary theory has explained the mystery of existence.' Life is too rich and demanding for such statements to be acceptable. The purpose is to encourage growth and perception, not to kill them, as these simple answers sometimes do, whether they are religious or scientific.

The Middle Years

Direct experiential life-themes are not childish things now to be put away. Most children, one hopes, will have mastered the basic skills; they are now ready to explore them more deeply and widely. The development of writing, of printing techniques, of spectacles and telescopes to aid sight, of telephones and radio to extend hearing, an awareness of a wider world which may be perceived through the microscope and the telescope, all these are of interest to the older junior child. In addition, his awareness of a past before he existed and a world beyond his present geographical horizons is beginning to intrigue him.

As he begins to look around him, the child also becomes conscious of the phenomenon of religion. Christmas and, in many cases still, Sunday School will have been part of his life, but not often in a personal religious sense—not, that is, in terms of conscious awareness. They have been part of the given way of life to be accepted and taken for granted. Now, however, he is beginning to ask questions, many but not all of them factual. Frequently parent and teacher are baffled because, although he can ask profound questions, he is not yet able to cope with the answers.

Religion at this stage, it is suggested, should be approached through the tangible, leaving 'why' questions until later, unless the individual child raises one, when the answer should be given to that child, as with younger children, but not yet to the class as a whole.

The Later Years

Many pupils will never reach the position of being able to master abstract theological ideas. This may be because of intellectual limitations; equally possibly the reason may be a lack of interest. This need not force the teacher as an alternative to an exploration *ad nauseam* of secularly confined themes on money, sex or leisure, often no less remote and arid than theology. Another approach might be attempted —that of grappling with the ultimate questions of life by beginning with life, not with theology or philosophy.

Myself invites the adolescent no longer to think first of all about developing physical senses but to think much more about emotions, power, purpose and to consider the question 'Who am I?' To some extent the answer is biological or historical or sociological; but religions wish to say something else, not something necessarily contradictory, perhaps something more. Humanists and atheists, whilst rejecting the transcendent in attempting to answer questions, also tend to see something extra in the human personality. Freedom of will, responsibility for his actions, the ability to manipulate his environment mark man out as more than a stage in evolution, responding conditionally. 'Who am I?' is a question certainly no less real to the Humanist than to someone who may reply, 'You are the child of God.' This is a proper question to be posed in the upper school and one which the pupil has a right to explore openly.

The second area of first-school work, *myself and others*, is what, in many upper schools today, appears to be the total content of religious/moral education. It is familiar enough to require only two comments here. First, the topics are often treated in a purely secular way. Perhaps because of the reactions of the teacher or class to religious belief and commitment, this has become accepted, inoffensive, neutral ground. Secondly, this approach can degenerate into a study of unrelated topics, the pupils frequently presenting at second hand the views of their parents or, occasionally, some television personality. It is well to remember that the great religions and many of the world's philosophers have also grappled with the relationships of man to society, but more important still is the recognition which most people have had for criteria by which to work out attitudes and responses to individual issues such as peace and war, race, political allegiance, punishment or choosing a job. Perhaps through a study of the way such men as Mahatma Gandhi, Dietrich Bonhoeffer, Martin Luther King, Trevor Huddleston or Muhammad Ali faced situations in which they found themselves questions of criteria might be raised, but care would have to be taken, as in the study of all great people, not to be remote. Most pupils will never lead civil rights campaigns; mixing with coloured workers on the shop-floor or expressing a minority opinion in the canteen may be their Salt March or Sophiatown, no less real, no less courageous and no less important even though history never notices their contribution.

Finally, returning to *myself and the cosmos*, one may study the various myths of creation and the coming of death and the answers which have been given to questions about man's nature and destiny. Here, again, religious and human interpretations have their place alongside those of science or sociology.

One hopes that in this section a rounded, coherent approach to what for sake of a more adequate term is called 'religious studies' has been provided. If not, it is hoped that friends and colleagues will use it in an attempt to construct something better, for a durable, adequate model for religious studies from 5 to 16 is urgently needed—one which is based not on religion or religions but on life.

The rest of this book is devoted to the examination of the way in which one aspect, world religions, may be developed within this framework.

Chapter 2

Approaching Someone Else's Beliefs—Some Criteria

If the changes now taking place in religious education are as successful as I would wish them to be, one result might be that my children or, more likely, my grandchildren will be taught about Christianity by a Jew or a Muslim. This is something far removed from the present situation in which the teacher is likely to be a Christian but may be someone of no commitment at all. As Muslims and Jews in Britain are aware, the crunch comes when their children are taught any beliefs by a member of an alien faith—and I use the word 'alien' intentionally to suggest the tension which exists, though in our arrogance many Christian teachers in multi-faith schools have acted with a complete disregard of it.

How might I ask a Jew or a Muslim to teach about the faith to which I am committed?

I think I'd begin by asking him to memorise those famous words of Max Warren's: 'Our first task in approaching another people, another culture, another religion, is to take off our shoes, for the place we are approaching is holy. Else we may find ourselves treading on men's dreams.' Christianity may not be the most holy path of all for him, but I am asking him when he is teaching about it to recognise what it means to me and to respect it as the trysting-place between God and myself. If he cannot, then he must not teach about it. In the same way, unless I can acknowledge that Humanism represents a meeting-place between some people and Existence just as significant and meaningful for them as Christianity is for me, I must leave the teaching of Humanism alone.

Descending from the high peaks of Max Warren's words to the class-room reality, I would ask my Muslim friend to teach as though I were sitting in the back row. In other words, there should be no gossip, no stories about a religion which would not be told in the presence of its adherents. Also, no advantage should be taken of childish ignorance. If the Muslim teacher had me sitting in front of him he would have to take care not to misrepresent the Trinity. In the same way, I should have to take care in teaching about the Crusades, the Muslim attitude to women or the permissibility of having four wives.

I'd want my Muslim friend to consult me, or at least to make use of reliable Christian books on worship and beliefs, so that he was able to present Christianity in its own terms, not his version of Christianity. He would have no difficulty in doing this, we might think, but it is surprising how few primers of Christianity exist which would make the faith intelligible to someone who stands outside it—as many children in our schools do, and not only those from Muslim or other faith backgrounds. As for myself, thankfully I can now go to books written by Muslims to learn about Islam, and to some extent I can use educationally sound text-books and audio-visual aids with pupils, thanks to the work of such people as Dr Muhammad Iqbal and Riadhe El-Droubie. Judaism has always provided the teacher with considerable assistance through the efforts for a long time of Myer Domnitz and the Jewish National Fund and more recently Rabbi Douglas Charing and the Jewish Educational Bureau. Sikhism has its Pam McCormack (formerly Wylam) and Piara Singh Sambhi. So far Hinduism and Humanism have lagged behind in providing teachers with reliable aids for use in the classroom.*

How helpful would I be to any Muslim wishing to present Christianity fairly to a class of 15-year-olds? Would I give him the Gospels and Acts plus a commentary and say, 'That's all you need'? This was the old approach, not yet replaced. Or would I give him some biographies of white Christian social reformers (often undoing the work of white Christian exploiters) and invite him to use those? Or would I supply him with a list of ethical problems and matching biblical texts? And, then, there are the denominations, of course! What help can we give a Muslim or a Humanist who is willing to help pupils understand what it means in terms of belief and practice to be a Christian? There is an urgent need for a re-appraisal of Christianity, but more of that later.

Granted that we have got the balance right and can present Hinduism as a Hindu would wish us to—a very difficult task incidentally, for many Hindus, whilst sharing in the 'folk religion', run it down in the presence of Westerners and present them with a sophisticated philosophical system as removed from Hinduism as a live faith as Barth's 'Dogmatics' is from Evensong—we must then ask the teacher to exercise his professional expertise in weighing the needs of the faith being presented against the understanding of the child being taught. Unless the Muslim who is teaching about Christianity does so in accordance with sound and proven educational principles, all his other good work, his attempts at fairness, his sincere approach,

*Some of the useful sources are:
The Jewish National Fund, Rex House, 4-12, Lower Regent Street, London SW1.
Minaret House, 9, Leslie Park Road, Croydon.
Jewish Education Bureau, 8 Westcombe Avenue, Leeds 8.

his efforts to understand Christianity on its own terms, will have been wasted. This especially requires the teacher to think carefully before telling stories of the birth of Jesus or the birth of Guru Nanak to 5-year-olds, and asks him to discriminate between cultural general knowledge and religious knowledge, between general education and religious education. Most Muslims in Britain today know the festival of Christmas as part of general education, and for some Christians Ramzan or Passover enjoy the same status; but, just as no Christian teacher worth his salary would attempt to explain the ideas behind Ramzan to 5-year-olds and tell them the whole narrative associated with it, so I must advise my Muslim teacher to take care in approaching Christmas or Easter with 5-year-olds. What would I ask him to do and teach? What would I teach 5-year-old Muslims about Christmas? Here, again, the Christian as a professional teacher has some questions to ask himself.

So far, for historical and religious reasons, RE has naturally been in Christian hands, and most of the research and study in this area of the curriculum has been undertaken by Christians. Gradually the situation is changing. The sauce of a faith being taught in a secular context by someone who may not personally be an adherent of it will be common to a Muslim goose or a Christian gander in future. This is a matter which must exercise Christians as much as Muslims and Humanists. It is something which I welcome, but so far not many Christians seem to have given this prospect much consideration.

Chapter 3

The Problem of Commitment

It is not difficult to *ask* a Christian teacher to keep his religious and philosophical convictions out of the classroom, and to teach in such a way as to give no one grounds for accusing him of using his unique position to indoctrinate the young. Should a teacher working in religious education doff his religious commitment before setting foot in the classroom? Is it possible that he *can*? It is difficult to see how any teacher could do this for long, even as an earnest of professional competence, however conscientiously he may try.

The firmer the commitment, the greater the reluctance to give an undertaking to profess neutrality. Part of the trouble at the present time is that the teacher is being asked to lead a kind of double life. With the best of intentions, he is invited to divide his life into a public compartment and a private one. The separation of private motivations from professional obligations is recommended as the best way of safeguarding the autonomy of his pupils and of promoting the development and integration of their personalities. There is a hint of irony here. If it is argued that this is not what is meant by separating personal religious commitment from professional responsibility, then it can only be said that those who take such a view have no clear idea of what religious commitment entails. Or perhaps it is because they are contending for a *different* kind of commitment.

It is well enough understood today that it is a sound educational principle to start where the child is (and, for that matter, where the teacher is). What, then, is the purpose of religious education and, in particular, of courses in world religions? Why introduce new 'languages' of greater and greater complexity into the lives of young people? My own observation suggests that many parents, teachers and others concerned with the education of the young are beginning to question the wisdom of trying to tackle so much in re-designed syllabuses. The real difficulties are obvious and practical. Under present arrangements too little time is provided in the curriculum for an increasingly demanding syllabus. Too much is expected of teachers who for the most part have not been equipped to deal with aspects of the major religions of the world in the classroom.

I do not see how anyone can reasonably take exception to the emphasis which is now placed on the need to safeguard the individual child from the dangers of doctrinal pressure from whatever source it may come. But this, of itself, does not resolve the difficulty. The progressive introduction of world religions into the curriculum makes it more than ever necessary to look at what is happening—if only to ensure that the repudiation of explicit Christian indoctrination does not, for want of vigilance, provide new opportunities for different but similarly exclusive world-views to take its place. It is not only Christian parents who take (what our pluralist society encourages them to consider as legitimate) exception to the content of some new syllabuses. In the past few months I have heard Muslims, Sikhs and Hindus criticise the way in which their faiths are being taught in schools. It is not the *principle* of pluralism to which they object. The objection is much more radical and potentially more destructive of the consensus approach to religious education which has developed during the last decade. It is that what is offered is *offensive*. It is not wilfully so. Many sincere teachers of other religions, such as the ones I have mentioned, would be distressed to hear that their best efforts were received in this way. If it were merely a question of factual ignorance, teachers would feel more able to cope with the criticism and take steps to make themselves better informed. It is not, however, their sincerity, but their *attitude* which is more often in question—at any rate, from the point of view of immigrant adherents of other religious faiths. A long tradition of scepticism and historical-critical inquiry has produced in the West an attitude which is wholly alien to the spirit of Islam, for instance. And what is looked upon as misrepresentation of their deepest religious beliefs by Muslims, Sikhs and Hindus is not, in the present situation, unknown to Christians and Jews either. One of the most frequent criticisms which I hear expressed by Muslim friends in this country is to the effect that, even where it can be said with justification that Western students of Islam take their studies seriously, it happens that what they study is a kind of Western construct which is scarcely recognisable to the Muslim community. Ignorance can be removed and attitudes can be changed, but it is painful for those of us who profess other faiths (or none) to be told that we so frequently fail to be fair. If this is in fact the case, it is hard to see how teachers can present religious systems for what they undoubtedly are—namely, systems of faith and belief which make great demands on the believer in terms of commitment and action. Still less is it possible to see how beleaguered teachers are expected to present these systems in such a way as to make possible, in due course, a personal choice from the options thus deployed, on the part of the individual child.

We have attempted to safeguard the interests of children in schools by encouraging openness in the *shared* search for truth. Not surprisingly, teachers are left wondering how they should go about this task. Like most of them, I would reject the idea that it is a teacher's job to proselytise. I have never defended the view that it is, and I can think of no circumstances in which I would be inclined to change my mind. On the other hand, experience has taught me that I have to start not only where children or students are, but also where *I* am, commitment and all. How is the teacher to proceed in what must be one of the most daunting tasks ever given to an educator? Not, it sometimes appears, out of the strengths and weaknesses of his own religious convictions and commitment. Appointing committees have a problem here, because unless they wish to debar certain candidates for posts in religious education they have to accept not only, for example, that committed Christians will seek such appointments in response to what they conceive to be a vocation, but also that it is only *out* of their religious commitment that they can proceed to do the job if it is offered. To suggest to a teacher that his professional duties oblige him to relegate his religious convictions to extra-curricular activities is to invite him to speak another's lines. This is not only a problem for the *Christian* teacher. The same applies to any teacher whose religious faith demands of him a total response to life. It simply fudges the issue to say that a Christian teacher can learn to work in a situation which may, in the words of C. B. Cox, 'introduce children to a culture actively opposed to Christian values'. He *may* be able to do this, but it is difficult to see how his response can escape charges of pragmatism and expediency.

My approach to the problems and opportunities which face teachers who are interested in the place of world religions in religious education is influenced by the conviction that it is only by a frank declaration of commitment and an open recognition of continuing religious and philosophical differences that we can come to the kind of tolerance and understanding which is the hall-mark of the open society. Anything less than this may support for a time an uneasy consensus approach to religious education, but in the long term it may do a real disservice to the children we teach. In any case, the cracks are already showing. I have it from someone who helped draft the Agreed Syllabus for Birmingham that criticism has come from at least two quarters. Predictably, it could be argued, criticism has come from groups of Christians who view with dismay the inclusion of sections dealing with Humanism and Communism. Equally predictably, it may be said, is the reaction of some Humanists who consider that the new syllabus remains disappointingly 'Christian' in content and spirit. These tensions are real, and are not eliminated by efforts to induce consensus by committee. Commitment that is dominating, exclusive and proselytising is generally considered to be inappropriate in the classroom. The commitment which I should like to see illuminating the school scene is that which is firm but provisional. Firm in that it represents a holding fast to what one *now* sees on the basis of the evidence examined *thus far*. To hear some teachers talk about open-ended inquiry is to gain the impression that every lesson begins *de novo*. It is provisional in the sense that it is open to change in the light of fresh evidence. Conversion thus becomes a stimulating prospect and loses its terror for anyone who is genuinely open to life.

This increased personal commitment to the truth as I see it takes me again and again into that potentially disturbing area of encounter with people from other religious traditions. There is no question of trying to compel assent to that which I hold to be true. It is more a matter of revealing my commitment so that anyone who is sufficiently generous to take it seriously may criticise and question it. Yet it would be dishonest if I pretended that by expressing my commitment I did not retain the hope that eventually some may even come to share it.

It is difficult enough to be landed with the teaching of a subject which is the only one in the curriculum to be demanded by law and the only one (in the absence of statistics about others) to be supported by over 90 per cent of parents. There is something encouraging about that last figure, but I sometimes wish that I had access to similar opinion polls which would demonstrate that even *one* other subject was comparably as popular. The reality is different. In spite of over-whelming public support, religious education continues to be criticised by pupils, parents and teachers alike, whether they are believers or not. New syllabuses, however imaginative their construction, will not, of themselves, change the situation. As one teacher put it to me recently with devastating simplicity, 'After three years of world religions the children are just as bored as they were with Christianity. What are we going to do about *that*?'

My chief purpose in this chapter is to encourage teachers of religious education who find themselves in a front-line position, alone at the front of a class, when all the in-service courses, conferences and seminars have finished, and when all the available books on the subject have been read. Study and discussion, particularly, in the wake of the analytical work done during the last decade, have made us think hard and question our assumptions. I have, nevertheless, felt increasingly in the past year or so that some important quality has been missing. It is as if some essential ingredient has been missing from the feast of ideas. It would be easy enough to say that what has been missing is *confidence*—by which I mean the confidence of the individual teacher of religious education in his own professionalism and in the importance of his subject within the framework of the total curriculum. It is scarcely surprising that confidence should have waned. Attacks have come from those who won't have religious education in state schools at any price. It is salutary to remember that they are still there and that they are likely to return to the fray. This kind of attack is predictable, sometimes justified in its detail, debilitating, but seldom totally destructive. It takes many forms, but is characterised by accusations to the effect that the teacher is imposing his own religious beliefs and value judgements upon children too young and inexperienced to defend themselves against indoctrination. It will be interesting to see in the next few years what new course the secular attack on religious education in state schools takes, in spite of the achievements of religious *détente* and the production of new syllabuses which recognise the religious pluralism of our society. Criticisms have also come from friends and sympathisers who continue to see religious education as the tool of mission, designed to ensure the transmission of the faith (whatever it may be) to the young.

In recent years many teachers have been asked to tackle aspects of their subject for which they have not been prepared. Not surprisingly, they have looked for guidance to experts in the field. In some instances this has led to a fascinating tangle. A teacher coming up to retirement put it to me this way: 'On one side there is the teacher, like me, with years of classroom experience, but puzzled about how he should introduce courses in "world religions". It is a subject in which I have a general interest, but little academic competence. On the other side stands the academic who discovers, not always to his entire peace of mind, that an expert knowledge of Qur'anic exegesis or the Pali canon or something even more technical has put him in a position in which he is increasingly asked to advise practising teachers whose classroom expertise he cannot match.' That there are notable exceptions to this does not take away from the general point. There are signs which seem to indicate that frustration increases as it becomes clearer that the experts themselves have little enough to offer other than native wit, personality and words of encouragement when it comes to dealing with practical classroom problems which face teachers every day. Who, in any case, *are* 'professional experts' in Christianity or Islam or Judaism or the other faiths by which men live? Teachers still feel obliged to consult those who *may* not know, from first-hand experience, what religious faith and commitment are.

I consider that the missing quality, to which I referred earlier, is *commitment*. I contend that to take religious education seriously the teacher must accept that children need help in the techniques of decision-making. This is not the same as teaching *for* 'decision', which, as we have noted, is inadmissible in a state school. Without education in *discrimination* between various religions and philosophical options (and no one pretends that in the interests of fairness they can *all* be examined), the deployment of those options is reduced to window-dressing. *Evaluation* cannot be avoided. The child who asks, 'But which one is right?' is more likely to be helped if the teacher has felt free to declare his own commitment and then to understand the implications of new beliefs and ideals for his own faith than by the teacher whose studied neutrality is, in effect, the expression of an impartiality which is alien to his deepest convictions.

It is important that the debate about religious education, and especially about the place of world religions in the syllabus, should be taken more seriously by everyone who professes to recognise the religious pluralism of our society. It does not surprise me that, in the reaction against traditional biblical approaches, members of other religious communities as well as secularists continue to argue for the elimination of *Christian* teaching and what they see as indoctrination. What *does* surprise me is that it should be thought that what was held to be unacceptable on educational grounds, as damaging to the autonomy of the individual child, should be replaced by something which is potentially no less tendentious. There is a fundamental ambivalence that needs to be challenged. It sometimes takes the form of recommending the removal of committed *Christians* from the classroom. The implication is that, having removed the indoctrinator from a place of influence, the school is now able to function in a more open fashion. Thus, in a college of education, for instance: 'My best students [of religious education] are atheists or agnostics'—presumably uncommitted atheists and agnostics at that. The statement has a certain old-world charm, but leaves me more sceptical than I would like to be about the education of the children whose teachers these students will presumably qualify to be.

Is it being seriously suggested that Muslims, Sikhs, Hindus, Jews and Humanists, either as parents of children in school or as teachers (or as both), have adopted as practical guide-lines for religious education in state schools the kinds of approach which are described in the following extracts from a subject-committee bulletin of the Schools Council? It may very well be that they *should*, but that is a different matter.

A great change in the concept of religious education has taken place in the last quarter of a century. The modern RE teacher is concerned to teach people to think, to question and to discuss, as against encouraging them to receive ideas and information passively, *the educational mode of former times*. The modern teacher is also concerned to extend the child's awareness to include many forms of man's religious strivings instead of concentrating on Christianity alone. *Another important change is that moral education is no longer regarded as synonymous with RE.*

This passage comes from a statement prepared by the British Humanist Association in 1970. I have italicised two parts of the extract which interest me. How far back do we have to go to find 'former times'? Are we to accept that children were not taught 'to think, to question and to discuss' before the advent of 'the modern RE teacher'? And, more to the point, what is the *evidence* which shows that, having arrived, 'the modern RE teacher' is really delivering the goods? The point about the distinction between religious education and moral education is, of course, a basic Humanist concern. As an expression of Humanist commitment the statement is clear, but it is unlikely to commend itself to Muslims and Sikhs, for example, for whom religion and morality are inextricably linked.

Another passage from the same Schools Council bulletin shows how much is being asked of the RE specialist who

poses and invites questions about the meaning of human life, and of the world in general. Is there meaning and purpose in the universe as a whole? And what difference to our attitudes and behaviour in particular circumstances does the answer to the general question make? The teacher will examine this enquiry with the aid of Christian and non-Christian statements. He will also examine the alternative—that there is no ultimate meaning in existence—and its implications. He will examine the nature of belief and the necessity for making a choice. . . . The choice itself remains the pupil's own; and the teacher should not measure the success of his teaching by the extent to which his pupils agree with him. What he is called on to do, as a teacher, is to make clear the available choices and the grounds thereof; and to help his pupils to make their choices and face the consequences of making them.

A more forbidding job-specification than that would be hard to imagine. It would surprise me to find many teachers who would be willing to lead such a dangerous life. Two things strike me about the extract which I have just quoted. The first is that it is unrealistic. There is something to be said for having an ideal at which to aim, but perfection of the kind advocated here is enough to make the noblest spirit droop. Consider the whole sweep of the thing, from 'questions about the meaning of human life' to the assertion that it is not only the 'alternatives', but also the 'implications' of those alternatives which are to be examined. The passage is typical of contemporary liberal orthodoxy. Nothing is omitted. The second thing which strikes me about it is that it contains no statement about the *motivation* of the teacher. The problem of commitment is reduced to carefully guarded statements about a variety of options which, to judge from the passage quoted, may be equally valid. Does his responsibility end when he has fairly examined the alternatives? If he decides that he cannot do justice to the options about which he has at least some idea, does he withdraw, leaving the field to polymaths who *can* cope? Who is to decide in a given case that a particular option has been treated fairly? And what help in evaluation and discrimination is to be given to the searching child?

The authors of the Schools Council Working Paper 36 also take a broad view of the subject. Their formulation seems to me to combine a more precise analysis with a recognition of the limitations imposed on teachers and children by the situations in which they have to work.

> We incline to the view that religious education must include both the personal search for meaning and the objective study of the phenomena of religion. It should be both a dialogue with experience and a dialogue with living religions, so that one can interpret and reinforce the other.... Religious education seeks to promote awareness of religious issues, and of the contribution of religion to human culture in general; it seeks to promote understanding of religious beliefs and practices; it also aims to awaken recognition of the challenge and practical consequences of religious belief. Like all liberal education it is concerned that such awareness and understanding should be founded on accurate information, rationally understood and considered in the light of all relevant facts.

This is a formidable programme. To make it work we need to know what the 'religious issues' are. We also need to know to what extent 'a dialogue with living religions' depends upon the availability of committed adherents of different faiths, and upon the welcome they will receive in schools, especially if they also happen to be teachers. This assumes greater importance in the light of the last sentence which has just been quoted.

For a long time now Christians have been the recipients of a great deal of criticism about the relationship between their personal faith and their professional responsibilities. It is as if their inability or unwillingness to differentiate were unique. Another aspect of ambivalence reveals itself here. It is not easy to avoid the feeling that, unless a reciprocal renunciation of explicit classroom commitment is pledged by the representatives of *all* the faiths and philosophies involved, we shall discover rather sooner than later that what passes for consensus is bogus.

Hindus, Sikhs and Muslims have pointed out with some justification that Europeans have misunderstood and misrepresented their faiths. It would be sad if, in the development of a more open and tolerant society, they were to use newly formed opportunities for self-expression to misrepresent or belittle *each other's* faith. Christians have found their commitment challenged and isolated. There is no reason why they should be expected to conform to a standard of professional conduct which does not apply to other religious groups. It is an open secret that many practising Hindus, Sikhs and Muslims, not to speak of Jews and Christians, fail to recognise the faiths which they profess in the courses provided by schools, colleges and universities. Part of the trouble lies in the fact that many of the courses are prepared and taught by Westerners who assume a prior commitment to openness and neutrality that is wholly bereft of the kind of commitment which characterises the faith of the believer. The way is open for misrepresentation. I cannot believe that the adherents of any of these faiths will continue to exercise restraint in the face of what they hold to be serious misrepresentation, even in the pursuit of co-operation in the field of education.

It is the superficiality of the treatment of religion which is so potentially disastrous. What can teachers expect to achieve in the time available? The desire to do *something* in spite of the limitations of time and knowledge tends to conceal the weakness of superficiality. I remember discussing this with a colleague who is an Arabist. He regretted that as year followed year he could expect nothing better than to wait for small groups of students who would, for a few terms (their courses allowed for little more), be given an 'Introductory Course in Modern Literary Arabic'. One wonders how many students ever progress beyond an introduction. The same might be said of world religions in school. It is not difficult to be endlessly busy about an annual cycle of 'introductions to . . .'. On his return from a visit to the United States, the publisher John Todd recorded some of his impressions in an article for the *Tablet*.

> By the end of my three weeks I was feeling rather sorry for many of the students who seemed to be swimming in a sort of warm sea of 'spirituality' without a landmark in sight. Very largely detached from conventional social structures they were faced with something like a great smorgesbord of religions; and one sensed the unreality of a situation where students were, one might almost say, committed to commitment. . . . It is difficult to find one's way where there are a hundred brands of theoretical religion on sale, and praxis largely theory too.

It is indeed difficult to find one's way where there are so many paths. It is made more difficult when the teacher is himself confused about why he is attempting to consider other religions. There is much to be said for embarking on what Roger Hooker has recently described as an 'Uncharted Journey', but it is interesting to note that his approach in Benares to the Hindu-Christian encounter is one which recognises the importance of religious commitment on both sides from the outset.

During the last decade there has been a lot of activity in the theory and analysis of religious education. The battle-cry of the mid-sixties, 'RE must go', is heard less and less without the camp (although some small bands come down from the hills from time to time, to remind us that it is still an issue). In so far as it is possible to find out, it seems that large numbers of parents and teachers would consider the curriculum impoverished if no place were to be found for religious education. It appears that this view is held by many different groups of people whose personal philosophies differ. It appears that believers in God, and non-believers too, have found common ground in an approach to an exploration of the spiritual side of man's nature. Whatever the mistakes of the past may have been, it would seem that the way forward looks less and less like a path across a battle-field. Sweetness and light.

How realistic is it to take the consensus at more than face value? Is it likely that individuals and groups from such widely different cultural, religious and philosophical backgrounds can for long pursue common educational aims? Or is it the case (and I have heard this view expressed more frequently of late) that the common-front approach of Humanists, Christians (lumped together for the purpose of the argument), Jews, Muslims, Sikhs and others serves only to conceal the very real differences of attitude and approach which are expressed privately? Real or imaginary, however, current orthodoxy in religious education rests on the assumption that such a consensus is both desirable and possible.

Philosophers, psychologists (though, unhappily, few theologians) have produced a library of analysis about religious education. There is much in the analysis to which I have been referring with which I agree, notably about the pluralistic society in which we live and the need to avoid indoctrination and to stimulate the religious quest. But my criticism of much of this research and the way its results are applied is much more one of attitude. I still detect far too little emphasis on what Huston Smith called 'religion as an acute fever'. There is still too much that is characteristic of 'dull habit'. My major criticism is based upon my observation that the programme which is frequently being advocated, particularly during the course of in-service training and in the not infrequent day-conferences to which teachers are invited, is too unrealistic. There is too much to be attempted in too little time.

I have been concerned in this chapter to bring into focus some of the issues that face the teacher as a result of his own religious and philosophical commitment. I have also wanted to challenge the assertion that the declaration of personal commitment on the part of the teacher is *necessarily* inimical to the processes of religious education. My contention is that the suppression of a teacher's religious convictions (or of his atheistic convictions, or of his leanings towards agnosticism) in the day-to-day discharge of professional obligations is impossible *in practice*. Procedural neutrality and an attempt fairly to examine alternative systems of belief and unbelief are not *necessarily* beyond the capability of such committed teachers to achieve.

It has not been my intention to attempt here the more exacting exercise of showing how the theology of the curriculum that I hold might be worked out in detail in state schools. This larger task is one that I am working on elsewhere, but I should like, in conclusion, to refer to some of the points which I consider need to be discussed further.

We need to look yet again at what is happening in state schools and to ask what religious education is for. I would say that the aim of religious education is to provide children with the knowledge and skills that will enable them, as they grow into maturity, to approach the phenomena of religious experience (and the possibility of personal religious commitment) in such a way as to indicate their increasing understanding of and sympathy for its various manifestations. But there is more to it. In my view, the aim is to make commitment in *any* of its many forms more *self-aware*. Much of the discussion about neutrality and objectivity in religious studies proceeds along lines which suggest that neutrality is thought of rather as a *method* than as a studied commitment in itself.

It is not the business of teachers to insist that a child decide for this faith or for that. Religious education is nonetheless a process in which growth and progress ought to be discernible. It ought to be possible to evaluate progress in religious education, but only if there is some prior conception of what the processes of religious education are designed to achieve. Two things seem to me to be worth saying at this point. First, that the personal commitment of the teacher (whatever it may be), far from being a professional liability, is an inescapable and indispensable primary resource. Secondly, that religious education is a continuing process of personal development which involves both teacher and pupil in a continuing quest for truth. In general terms (there is not space for a fuller analysis here) it seems necessary to recognise that personal growth and development call for something more specific than a theoretical acknowledgement of religious pluralism. The teacher has a unique opportunity to convert the theory into practice at *the personal level*. The teacher has the chance to demonstrate how (if at all) the existence of an alternative belief system modifies his own commitment, and in concrete terms to encourage his pupils to question the assumptions of their own existing commitment. The teacher may choose to illustrate this by bringing to the discussion such information as he may be able to glean from other faiths, but he will not be deluded into thinking that he is thereby 'teaching' world religions. He has, in my view, a profounder aim, which is to establish within practical limits a dialectical tension between the poles of his own declared commitment and that of another faith or life-stance that is opposed to his own. This willingness to be seen to be vulnerable is the prerequisite for any teacher who sees religious education attended by the dynamics of personal growth.

To this end there is a need to prepare the kind of material which will provide opportunities for progress in religious sensitivity and aware-ness in ways which, in some respects, may be analogous to the ways by which literacy and numeracy are developed in other parts of the curriculum. Are Christians (or for that matter Muslims, Sikhs and others) for ever excluded from constructing and articulating a theology of the curriculum as a contribution to the open society on the grounds that their commitment disqualifies them from effective membership? Is the open society one in which the guardians declare that there are more fundamental educational principles which are logically prior to any consideration of the implications of religious belief with reference to education, and to which the requirements of religious belief must ultimately be subordinated? Are these educa-tional principles to remain inaccessible to the criticism of the various theologies of the curriculum? If so, it would seem that the position of specifically 'religious' education in state schools has been considerably weakened. The term 'religious education' is seen to be as redundant (or as mischievous), as the term 'Christian education' or 'Muslim education'. No Christian or Muslim can subscribe to the view that his faith has no worthwhile contribution to make to the education of the child. The almost totalitarian way in which our society gives evidence of a refusal to submit its own presuppositions to the scrutiny of a Christian theology of the curriculum is an index of the way in which a commitment that purports to be procedurally neutral soon becomes invested with the characteristics of a dogmatic and exclusive quasi-religion. It may be argued that it is not the least important part of the function of religious education to make those who subscribe to such a view of education more aware of the nature of their own particular brand of commitment.

Chapter 4

Please, Sir, Do You Believe in God?*

A teacher may well be subjected to all manner of children's questions and comments:

> How do you spell your name?
> You look funny without your glasses!
> Where did you go for your holidays?
> Have you got a girlfriend?
> If your wife died, would you marry again?
> Do you believe in God?

These are often ingenuous, but they can also be devastating in their directness. Nice neutrality can be caught off guard! How to respond to such questions is therefore a problem for any teacher, especially so when matters of personal beliefs and values are involved.

Of course, the problem may be illusory once the question itself has been properly understood. This is illustrated by the fable of the 8-year-old asking his teacher how John Stephens got here. The teacher, not wishing to be bashful or reticent about sex education, seizes the opportunity to explain the biological facts of conception and birth. The children listen attentively, and that is the end of that. Until, that is, five minutes later when the same little boy asks, 'But, Miss, how *did* John Stephens get here?' It then emerges that he has recently learned that his friend John used to live in Australia.

A theological equivalent of this situation would be for a teacher to answer the question 'What makes flowers grow?' by immediate reference to God. Though in some final sense the teacher might be personally convinced of the dependence of the world and all that in it is upon God, it would be quite inappropriate to give this as a direct answer to a child's question. For, very likely, the child will have been primarily concerned with how it is that today there is a flower, when a few weeks ago there was nothing showing above the surface of the soil. If the teacher finds it difficult to answer the question, appeal to God as a way out will only confuse the issue. It may give temporary respite from the child's questioning, but it will not be long before the question becomes 'Who made God?' Far better, let the teacher explain the dependence of the flower on water and sunlight, and perform small experiments with bean-sprouts with and without water and light. This will not give a complete answer, either, to the original question, but it will go part of the way towards revealing something of the complexities of the process involved and perhaps be the occasion for further wondering about life.

Before any attempt is made to answer a child, therefore, it is vital to find out what the questions mean in their own terms. Otherwise, all manner of category-mistakes can be made in response.

It may be that misunderstandings of this kind are happily rare. The major problem remains, however: 'Please, Sir, do you believe in God?' What is the teacher to respond when directly faced with a personal theological question such as this?

In spite of any temptation to give testimony, an immediate answer 'Yes' or 'No' will probably be unhelpful. Even though the risk of category-confusion may be smaller here than in the case of the previous question, sensitivity to what is motivating the child's inquiry is important. For instance, it may be that the boy or girl asking it is simply wishing to get to know more about the teacher. The question is then on a footing with 'Where did you go for your holidays?' It is semi-personal, seeking to extend the basis on which the child can relate to an older person. Thus, a teacher sensing the presence of such other motives may subsequently seek to multiply the occasions when the individual child can enter into a talking relationship with a trusted adult. This general security of mutual understanding should then make expressly theological exchanges all the more intelligible.

There is a danger, however, that deliberate reticence in theological matters may quickly give the appearance of evasiveness. Nothing in the classroom is more dishonest than the teacher who prises from the children the more intimate of personal disclosures, while (somewhat voyeuristically) refusing to reveal his or her own private depths. Even an appeal to an educational doctrine of neutrality is no licence for a teacher to be less than fully personal in the classroom. I have no excuse for dodging children's questions when they come.

Yet the questions themselves do require translation before they can be properly understood. Sensitivity to context is an important aspect of any translator's art, and especially so here. In the first place there is the child's own context, and secondly there is that of religion and theology.

The child's context has already been mentioned. 'Non-theological' motives and interests may at times be primary, even in questions framed in the most theologically loaded language. Where this is obviously not the case, such other motives and interests may at least accompany what really is intended as a theological question. For the subtleties and associations which we pack into words are rarely available from a straightforward lexical analysis of the formation of words used. But in addition there is a further sense in which the child's own theological context has to be understood. From first exposure to talk of God and other institutional religious language, children build their own idiosyncratic appreciations of the vocabulary involved. More than likely, this will be personally coherent, but its relation to public theological discourse will be personally peculiar. I well remember a 6-year-old girl talking to me at some length about 'God's sins'. It eventually became clear that she was consistently using the word 'sins' instead of the more usual word 'spirits'. Less blatant nuances of meaning may be more difficult to detect, but are no less important if a child's thoughts are to be properly appreciated. In any one class of children, therefore, the different understandings of 'God-talk' will be manifold.

This would be true even in a cultural situation which is relatively monochrome. Diversities of theological understanding even within an exclusive sect can yet be considerable. But our increasingly multi-cultural society in England and the diversity of the wide world daily infiltrate the lives of every boy and girl. They do this through books and television, as well as through contact with friends and families who think differently—'migrants' in a physical or a philosophical sense. Deliberate questioning about belief in God on the part of any child can still, therefore, come from many different directions.

How well he understands the direction of each child's questions is a crucial test of professional sensitivity. Without it, a teacher will not know what he is saying 'Yes' or 'No' to, when he responds. It could even be that his own belief were the child's unbelief, or vice versa.

Theology's own context makes similar demands on personal under-standing. Religious language is variously found in jokes and oaths, in creeds and atheistic manifestoes, in prayers and personal confessions. Excess of use, or the apparent babel of many different belief systems, can lead to the response that 'God is dead'—killed, as it were, by an inflationary spiral of words. Sensitivity is required to translate the in-tended significance of a theological currency, newly minted or debased.

Comparable difficulties occur in respect of human sexuality. Language deals with sex in ways superficial and profound; its intimacies can similarly be debased by sentimentality or brutality. 'God-talk' and 'sex-talk' alike thrive on personal centres of meaning, and words can both protect and trespass there.

'Please, Sir, do you love your wife?' or 'If your wife died, would you marry again?' are immediately recognisable as highly personal questions. Yes or no answers could be given, but the hesitations which might occur instead probably indicate that full-frontal frankness runs the risk of diminishing the richness of the personal intimacy involved. Questions about belief in God are no less intimate and personal. Depending on context, they too may be ruled out of bounds, but to be answered at all in school they require very careful treatment.

The fact is that there are many different ways of believing or dis-believing in God. A major priority in school, therefore, is to encourage boys and girls to explore for themselves the meanings of belief and unbelief, to bring their own preliminary questions and affirmations about life into relation with those of others and to learn from the exchange. How to do this is the problem of answering the child's question.

Exposure to a factual description of the religious experience of man-kind—theistic and atheistic—is fundamental. Just as biological facts have an important part to play in sex education, so too have the religious facts of life in religious education. Thus, a teacher may set out in detail that so many people believe in God in, for example, Catholic, Hindu or Jewish ways, and so many believe in a secular Humanist, Maoist or Buddhist way. He may then go on to describe their respec-tive trappings, where they are to be found in the world, and how they have developed there. All this will be preliminary groundwork.

Actually to know what it might mean to be a religious believer or unbeliever also demands a further imaginative working with the basic information, which might otherwise remain inert. Only then are many of the factual aspects of religion revealed as vehicles of inter-subjective claims and insights, deserving to be met as such.

In order to represent the vitality of any one tradition, the teacher will draw sympathetically on the artefacts of faith—special books and rituals, temples and meeting-places, fasts and festivals, creeds, codes of behaviour, and visual imagery. Pupils and teacher together reach to find the pulse of meaning that throbs within these artefacts.

This reaching will make demands familiar to anyone who has tried to make some aspect of history or literature come to life. It may well entail encounter with points of view so strange as to be alien.

The teacher's personal beliefs do not alter the facts of this situation—it exists independently of him. In seeking to introduce boys and girls to its fullness, the teacher will have the advantage, however, of both greater personal maturity and professional training. For the purposes of furthering their understanding, therefore, he will seek to mediate the intricacies and tensions of beliefs, and to do this most effectively he may need to be as a Christian or a Muslim or an atheist, for example. Thus the actual richness of a specific belief that thrives in the world today may be more fairly represented.

Taking on different stances of faith as an aid to teaching and learning will demand something of an actor's art. During school years teachers and children regularly play the parts of wolves, dragons, deceivers, even murderers, yet without the identification becoming so complete a fixture that their original identities are lost. And they grow as persons in this dramatic process. Similarly, by meeting or mating with different religious identities, each individual may deepen his or her own.

Thus, different answers to the question 'Do you believe in God?' quite properly deserve to be heard by the children, even from the same teacher. The greatest danger that can arise from this, perhaps, is that of confusion, but fortunately it is not inevitable. Provided that the different beliefs are related to specific groups of people, children need be no more confused about this than about differences between one family's life-style and that of another, between living on a farm and growing up in an inner city, or between membership of one political party and another. Nor will the teacher wish to contort himself into espousing all the different identities at once. On occasion, however, it will be appropriate for the teacher to 'play' a particular believer's role, so that the children may be given opportunity to come to terms with the diversities of belief in a productive educational context.

Commitment is an important criterion for any teacher engaging in this process—commitment, that is, to taking the religious and a-religious experience of mankind seriously, rather than to any predetermined theological persuasion. This will be a professional commitment—an educational virtue in the first instance; though, according to the traditional pursuits of tolerance and truth in religious tradition, potentially also a theological one.

The professional commitment coupled with a teacher's personal integrity is the real guarantee that the question 'Do you believe in God?' will be fairly answered. But in addition, each teacher will almost certainly have his or her own individual version of belief or unbelief of varying intensity, for this is a fundamental expression of personal identity. Admission of personal conviction in response to a child's question in the end needs no apology, therefore, but the meaning of the answer can ever have only the appearance of simplicity. For secreted within will be the great ambition that the children will in their own time find their ways of answering that self-same question for themselves.

Relevant Reading
I. G. Barbour, *Myths, Models and Paradigms: the Nature of Scientific and Religious Language* (SCM Press, 1974).
D. Bonhoeffer, 'On Telling the Truth', in *Ethics* (Fontana, 1964).
J. Britton, *Language and Learning* (Penguin, 1970).
D. Miller, *New Polytheism* (Harper and Row, 1974).
D. Solle, 'The True Teacher', in *Christ the Representative* (SCM Press, 1967).

PART TWO SOME PRACTICAL CONSIDERATIONS

The first group of essays relates to questions of approach and the use of materials, whether they be religious objects or stories. The second discusses Marxism, Buddhism and Christianity. Marxism is a subject of contention. Some teachers would admit that it should be taught, but as part of the history syllabus. Would it then be emasculated of its ideological aspects—as the Crusades, for example, are often presented without any reference to Islam? Whatever one's views about Communism as a political system, it is perhaps the most influential force in today's world, and we must ask ourselves whether children can be considered properly educated if they leave our schools ignorant of its world view as well as of its history.

An essay on Buddhism is offered partly because of the nature of that faith, but also because no person or group—not even the Shap Working Party—has yet addressed itself to the subject in print.

I may have been a little defensive in writing a piece on Christianity, sometimes being cast in the role of justifying world religions against (by implication) Christianity. On the contrary, I am very concerned that children should be taught about it, but just as they learn about Islam or Judaism, as a multi-dimensional living faith. The practical task is more difficult partly because of the teacher's and pupils' relationship to the Christian faith. The teacher is likely to be committed to it and eager to avoid the charge of being an evangelist, or he has rejected it and feels uneasy, almost guilty, or he finds it hard to make it something other than Bible-study. For his pupils it is the church on the corner to which their parents no longer go.

Chapter 5

Why World Religions—and Which?
A Beginning, a Middle and an End

It might seem an absurdly obvious truism to resort to a Joadian expression and say the inclusion of world religions all depends on why you are teaching RE—as does selection. However, the remark needs to be made, for so many teachers seem to include one of four religions in addition to Christianity with little thought.

If the purpose of RE is to induct pupils into the Christian faith, there would appear to be no place for teaching about any other religions unless it were to show how Christ vanquished Mithras or how Christianity is superior to Buddhism. Anyone with such aims should leave other religions alone; they do not exist to provide ammunition of this sort, which nowadays might blow up in the teacher's face, and I personally would prefer such a person to become an ordained minister or a teacher in a denominational school.

Where the aim is to understand the place and function of religion in human experience it can still be argued, quite correctly, that this can be done through the study of Christianity. In fact, those who talk about 'Christ in Hinduism' or 'Christ in Islam' are really saying that any sublime insights which these faiths may possess are to be found in Christianity, and it might be argued, therefore, why go to Hinduism or Islam to find them? If, holding this view, a teacher began to explore the total multi-dimensional richness of Christianity, its rites, its art, its diversity of worship, its insights as well as the Bible, such a course could only be applauded and held up as an example for others to copy. Would it be sufficient? I would wish to argue its inadequacy in a number of respects. First, it implies that Christianity is the only religion worth knowing about. This is a form of unintentional evangelism, seen from a Muslim or Humanist viewpoint. Something the child can easily conclude is that if he doesn't learn about it in school it isn't worth knowing. Secondly, it is unreal in terms of the late-twentieth-century world. Television, not only in the religious slots, but also in plays, has shown aspects of Jewish or Muslim life, and the number of documentary programmes about other cultures is increasing. Even if this multi-faith community is not with us in the form of a boy wearing his turban and sitting in front of us, it is increasingly present in these other ways, and the time has come to recognise it in the curriculum. One might add two other arguments.

One, frequently put forward is 'Who knows England, who only England knows?' That is, the familiar is so much with us that we cannot see it, never mind see it in perspective. Also, we are so close to it that we cannot view it with detachment. A good example here is that of the miracles of Jesus as opposed to those of Guru Nanak. Students have been known to reject those of the Indian out of hand whilst defending those of Jesus and being a little uncertain about those of his Hebrew antecedents. More pertinent in the school context is the way in which someone who has observed worship in a gurdwara sometimes comes to his week-by-week Christian worship with fresh insights, and by extension sees the whole concept of worship as more meaningful and profound. This isn't to suggest that one should teach Sikhism to make Christianity better understood; but the understanding of Sikh worship can contribute to a discovering of the meaning of worship as a whole, and this is likely to prompt a more reflective attitude to Christian worship. A further argument for including other religions besides Christianity is that by studying it alone we may be dulling the senses and the mind. All subjects are boring to some pupils, and often I suspect that RE comes off worst only because no one has bothered to ask about English Literature or Maths; but allegations must also be taken seriously, and it is possible to cover the life and teaching of Jesus with 12- or 14-year-olds, using Luke's gospel as the text, so that at the end of the year they have no portrait of Jesus and only an impression of the theological ideas Luke was wishing to communicate to the reader. I'm sure it can be done. I fear I have done it myself! Despite my jokes and charts of Holy Week (which still deserves capital letters if Ramzan does), some pupils were bored and few saw the purpose of the exercise, either mine or St Luke's. If we have to prune our syllabuses to provide some place for Buddhism, it might help us to sharpen our focus on Christianity and present it more satisfactorily. The question 'What must go?' which I am frequently asked may be one which we should all be attempting to answer. It should not be thrown down as a challenge, but like one of the queries and advices sometimes used at the beginning of a Quaker meeting it should provide an opportunity for self-reflection. Is the aim to understand Christianity or possess extensive biblical knowledge—though the extent of this often stops short of those mighty epistles, Romans and Hebrews? A course aimed at understanding religion must explore all the dimensions of religion and also indicate something of the many religious systems which exist.

The reasons for including Humanism and Marxism can vary from the polemical to the demand for fairness. Here I mention only three. First, if we are helping the pupil in his search for meaning we must not predetermine the limits and say that his solution will be religious. He should, therefore, be given some understanding of how people can work out their place in existence without reference to religion. Humanism provides such a coherent alternative view of life. So does Marxism, and it is also the most dynamic belief system of the twentieth century. Somewhere in the curriculum pupils should be able to learn about it fairly. Because RE deals with beliefs as no other subject does, this would seem to be an appropriate place for it, which is a second reason. Besides realism, intellectual honesty seems to require the RE teacher at least to recognise that people do make sense of life without having a religious belief. This is a third reason for including Humanism or Marxism, but I would hope the teacher would not treat them as reluctant afterthoughts! The supermarket best-buy is not a reason at all! I do not believe that people choose their beliefs in this way. A child from a Christian home is more likely to become a Humanist because of his home and its attitude to religion and to him or because of society at large than as a result of learning about Humanism in RE. A Muslim or Jewish child's identity problems will come not from RE but from being a member of a minority community in Britain. It must be conceded that the inclusion of Humanism and its fair and adequate treatment can result in the pupil inferring that it is worthy of respect. I happen to think that it is, and that Marxism is too. Of course, those who wish to restrict RE to religions will presumably exclude Humanism and Marxism.

How far is the list to be extended? To Mormons and Jehovah's Witnesses? These are religions. I see no reason for stopping short of them except pressure of time and the danger, as some might see it, of making them appear respectable. The first might be a legitimate reason for exclusion, so long as we are perfectly honest about our motives. In an open society I cannot accept the second—if pupils are to understand religion there seems to be a strong case for examining these new faiths of the Christian West in the same way that we approach Islam or Christianity, discovering what they say and claim, and why they came into existence and how their adherents interpret existence and find meaning. In the same way a place could be argued for witchcraft, but not to titillate or for the teacher to appear 'way out'. Why modern man turns to transcendental meditation or the ouija board is surely a proper question for RE at an appropriate stage. The criterion of selection will arise again, in the next sub-section.

A BEGINNING, A MIDDLE AND AN END

The Teacher
By now readers of this book should be aware that the task they are engaged in is one which demands serious thought. It is easy and

apparently tempting to have an affair with the first religion which comes along. The Prayer Book's warnings about marriage, 'not to be enterprised, nor taken in hand, unadvisedly, lightly or wantonly', are not inappropriate to someone considering teaching world religions, and in this category Humanism and Christianity are included. The teacher must possess accurate knowledge of the religion, and this means knowing it on its own terms. A Christian view of Islam or a Humanist view of Christianity is not enough. Also, he must know where the priorities come. The Torah and the Qur'an, not Moses and Muhammad, might be described as the Jewish and Muslim equivalents to Jesus, for example, since it is in them that God has supremely revealed himself. He must also have decided in his own mind what his over-all purpose is in teaching RE, why he had decided to teach about the interpretation of life which he is about to examine, and then have asked himself whether he has the necessary audio-visual aids as well as text-books.

Right knowledge, right attitudes, right intentions and right equipment might be regarded as the prerequisites of teaching world religions. This can be seen quite clearly by comparing the views expressed in the last paragraph with this quotation from the Sunderland Syllabus of 1944 which found a plan for world religions long before the Shap Working Party existed. After suggesting a fifth or sixth-form study of a variety of faiths from Judaism, through the ideas of Socrates, Aristotle, Buddha, Muhammad and modern Humanism, it concluded as follows:

> this review of the great religions of the World should lead us to see whatever is good in these religions in the conception of the character of God and man's duties is found unified and elevated in the Christian religion. Thus the practical goodness of Confucius, the valiant courage of Islam, and the contemplative patience of Hinduism or Buddhism all have their place in the revelation of God's character and man's duties in the life which was lived among men in Palestine 1900 years ago. Christianity, moreover, provides something which no other religion affords—a Saviour from sin and a present source of power and strength.
>
> It tends to unite all men in one great brotherhood under the loving God who is the Father of all alike, which is surely the desire of all nations and is destined to be the faith cf all mankind.

This reason for studying other faiths is now generally rejected by writers on RE and syllabus conferees, but the method, the emphasis upon beliefs unrelated to practices, lingers on. Reasons are not difficult to find. This has been the normal approach of colleges and universities in the past. It is the way that Christianity has been mistaught in schools, as biblical stories followed by biblical theology, possibly with some church history added. It is the grammar-school approach to education—text-books, notes and essays. Pictures and radio programmes are only for the secondary-modern child! The Cowper-Temple clause prohibiting denominational catechisms and formularies, and requiring that school worship shall not be distinctive of any denomination, may also have discouraged the study of religious practices. Traditional puritan attitudes to ritual may also have played their part.

Those who would teach world religions to children must, I think, shrug off the past and change not only their attitude but also their methods—that is, if they wish to present a religion to children as something which human beings practise and believe in, and which helps them to find meaning in life, as opposed to presenting them with a theological system, something completely cerebral.

Starting Out in World Religions
The clue to finding a satisfactory starting-point lies in the previous sentence. The practices of a faith, in its broadest terms, seem to be the natural place to begin because they relate so closely to things which some families still do, like going to church or celebrating festivals, or to feelings which are shared by all children—those of joy, thankfulness, excitement, even anxiety.

A start might be made with a Hindu, Muslim, Jewish, Buddhist, Sikh or Christian family. One might begin in Britain. If this is where one starts with a Jewish family, it should be possible with Buddhist or Sikh counterparts. However, in the latter cases, and with Hinduism and Islam, there may be a need quite early in the course to move to India, Pakistan or Thailand. There are good, though not overwhelming, reasons for placing the family in its traditional cultural environment. However, it is not only the contrast in food, climate and dress which is the teacher's concern; it is also the way a child is received into the family and community at birth, the celebration of weddings and festivals, and the relationship of the individual to his family and community of faith.

This will quickly lead to the mosque or church, other possible starting-points and with younger children initial stopping-points, perhaps.

The movement through family life, culture, festivals and ritual to beliefs may be swift with sixth-formers or students in further or higher education, perhaps occupying no more than two or three periods; but experience suggests that it is desirable, if not necessary. It is possible to understand Muslim philosophy and theology without ever meeting a Muslim or knowing how significant the Five Pillars and the Qur'an are in his life, but it is to be doubted whether such a student thus educated understands Islam.

Many of the religious texts which contain the foundation material for doctrines also provide a design for living and explanations of ritual practices such as sacred meals or festivals. It might seem best, therefore, to approach the Bible, the Guru Granth Sahib or the Qur'an less as a book full of stories (which none of them really is) and more as the revered literature of a community. The Sikh, Muslim and Jewish scriptures at least begin to be understood only when one sees how they are handled and regarded in the place of worship and in the homes of those adherents who possess them. This pupils might be helped to appreciate before they begin to use them as quarries for obtaining information of various kinds.

There is also a need to consider with some thought how the lives of important persons are to be taught. The biblical material about Moses or Jesus and the similar biographical information about Muhammad or Guru Janak have a theological content which is more significant than the simple narrative usually told to children. For example, the description (Mark, 2) of Jesus healing the paralysed man is not an example of brotherly love (on the part of his friends) or of compassion (on the part of Jesus) or an opportunity to discuss psychosomatic illness (on the part of the teacher) so much as a messianic proclamation. Perhaps in teaching about Jesus specialist teachers do now analyse their material and attempt first to present a portrait of Jesus as a man and later to say what Christians believe about him. The same awareness needs to be exercised in teaching about Buddha or Muhammad.

However, finally and essentially there is the doctrinal dimension and the element of personal commitment which is present in all interpretations of life. The latter may have been noted many times during the RE course: 'Christmas is a great time for everyone, but for Christians there is an added ingredient...'; 'The story of Rama and Sita is captivating, but to the Hindu...'; 'It is interesting to know what Jews do at Passover, but for the Jews the festival means...' Pupils will have realised that for the committed festivals, sacred books, Muhammad, Jesus or the Buddha have significance as well as interest—and that this is related to faith. However, there seems to be a place in the course for giving commitment special attention, and for showing that this is an essential part of Humanism or Marxism as well as of Christianity or Islam.

Unless such doctrines as God, life after death, salvation/liberation, and revelation are covered the course is incomplete. What sense is there in hearing about mosques or the positions of prayer in Islam unless one goes on to ask what worship is, what purpose it serves and what value it has? There is a similar illogicality in describing the rites or ethics of Christians or Sikhs if at the end no attempt is made to show how members of these faiths find meaning and interpret existence. Inevitably there will be expressions of scepticism as well as uncertainty; no teacher or teenager can be unaware that society is pluralist in its beliefs and values. Those who have studied world religions and such topics as worship, revelation or God will also be aware that beyond Christianity there are many other religions which claim to be the result of divine revelation, while within Christianity they will have encountered the non-sacramentalist Society of Friends as well as the liturgical richness of the Mass. They must also know that there are others, Humanists if not Marxists, who do not accept the claims of religion but who possess coherent world views upon which they base their lives. It is to be hoped that by the time pupils end their school days, at 16 or 18, they will be able to listen to what Humanists or Muslims have to say and be willing positively to appreciate how a variety of people understand themselves, the cosmos and their relationship to it and to others. Only then, one might argue, are they equipped to embark upon their own search for meaning in a pluralist world.

What Should We Include?
The progression suggested so far is:

(1) The social domestic culture;
(2) The religious practices;
(3) Important persons and the attitudes to religious texts;
(4) Major beliefs—selected with regard to the way they seem important to the student as well as being important within the faith.

The question now arises: Which religions should be taught? Tribal African, Polynesian, modern Japanese religious movements, Maoism, the Mormons, the Bahai faith—where do we stop?

Criteria of selection are required as much here as in teaching history, geography, mathematics or about Christianity.

Here are some.

(1) The teacher's own knowledge.
(2) The teacher's own inclinations. We have in mind the person who chooses to teach the subject, not the amateur with no specialist knowledge. No one can know everything, and some people may have a greater knowledge of and enthusiasm for, say, Hinduism

than Chinese religions. Let the teacher develop his strengths. In a school with two or three specialists it should be possible to provide variety and depth. Here a Christian or Muslim who feels he can only teach about his own faith can make his full contribution.

(3) The availability of teaching aids. To possess one picture of the present Dalai Lama and to be able to describe his flight from Tibet is an example of being inadequately equipped to teach about the religion of that country, yet teachers do it!

(4) The local, national or world-wide importance of a religion. On this basis, in Britain Christianity scores three times, Islam perhaps twice in most areas, Buddhism normally once, because of its place as a world religion.

(5) The contribution which the study of a particular faith can make to an understanding of religion.

(6) The contribution which the study of a faith can make in assisting pupils in their own search for meaning.

Individual teachers may wish to add other reasons of their own. They have then to put them together and work out some sort of syllabus which satisfies the criteria. Of course, we can all plead for our own specialism to be included. Someone once suggested taking the heat out of the multi-faith classroom by studying Buddhism! A Christian specialist in Old Testament studies once argued with me that in academic terms one could learn all about the places and function of religion by examining Hebrew religion to 70 CE. One hopes teachers will let common sense and their professional judgement overrule the arguments of specialists, be their interests Buddhist, Zoroastrian or Sikh!

Spurious criteria are to be avoided, such as the use of some traditional religion of Africa or America, living or dead, to pour scorn on superstition and to show how Christianity brought light or to show the folly of all religions. Or teaching about Buddhism and avoiding Christianity so that the teacher need not be embarrassed by his own beliefs being questioned or dismissed. Personal attitudes ought not to influence education in this way, but one knows of teachers who have said, 'It's easy teaching RE now. You just teach world religions. You don't have to believe anything yourself.' Three other reasons to be included in this category are the availability of a film-strip on Islam, a Jewish boy in the class, or a local Humanist willing to visit the school. Each can occasion a one-night stand with neither antecedents nor issue, indicative of a lazy teacher.

The reader might hope to be presented with a neat syllabus at this point. Instead he is offered this minimum:

(1) The pupil by 16+ should know what it means in terms of belief and practice to be a Christian and have some understanding of the contribution which Christianity has made to Britain and the world. (I argue the priority of Christianity on cultural grounds: in Pakistan I should give this place to Islam; in Israel to Judaism.)
(2) He should possess similar knowledge of one other major religion, and a general knowledge of a number of religions.
(3) He should understand how people with no religious beliefs—probably Humanists—interpret life, and know of the contribution which they make to human welfare and knowledge.
(4) He should possess a general knowledge of the main questions with which religions deal, and the answers which they offer.
(5) He should possess the equipment (both attitudes and skills) necessary for studying some other belief system which he has not even heard of in school should he later wish to.

This is in part a concession to practical considerations. I become increasingly aware that the body of knowledge in every subject is so vast that the knowledge explosion has scarcely begun to hit the classroom. As it does, factual information will become the servant of attitudes, skills and techniques. Numbers (3), (4) and (5) on the above list will assume priority over (1) and (2). However, just as a carpenter must develop his skills by working on wood, so the raw materials of belief systems will always supply the content through which teachers will seek to develop the pupils' awareness of and sensitivity to human experience and the various interpretations of it which the human mind and heart have employed and still do to make sense of it.

A SUMMARY

In tabular form the world religions syllabus might appear something like this.

Five stages	*World religions content*
(1) The child's own experiences.	NONE, except folk religion—i.e., the festivals and customs with which the child comes in contact. For most this still means Christmas trees and Easter eggs. Increasingly it is including turbans, clothes, food and Diwali celebrations.
(2) The descriptive and informative: largely a gathering of information—very much thematic, e.g., India, journeys,	What people do at festival times; what life is like in India today or in a Jewish home; Jesus' day; what the Bible or Qur'an is; Jesus, Guru

power, light, festivals, rather than exploring one culture in one direction.

Nanak or Gandhi, as a man; churches, synagogues, etc.; birth, weddings and funerals; topics exploring caring or the senses. Find a place for stories from a variety of faiths, of black people and white, women and men, Humanists and religious people.

(3) The meaning of things covered in 2 or (to avoid repetition) things similar at the level of initial impact and impression—still largely cross-religious.

What Bar Mitzvah means to a Jewish boy, or confirmation to a Christian. Believers' attitudes to the Bible or Qur'an. How atheists have depicted Jesus and why. The significance of aspects of Christian or Hindu worship, but of specific acts of particular faiths. The meaning of the Hajj or prayer to Muslim. Some religious stories and their significance.

(4) The underlying concepts.

Christian teaching about the person and work of Jesus. Concepts of God in the religions which have been studied, also worship, suffering, death and the life beyond. Key principles of belief and conduct.

(5) Bringing things together:
   (*a*) a coherent picture of the faiths studied.

What it means to be a Humanist, Christian, etc. The significance of commitment—perhaps through study of a faith or of people, e.g., Gandhi, Bonhoeffer, a Muslim family, as case-studies representing some aspects of practice and belief.

   (*b*) ultimate questions; making sense of life.

Why am I here? (A recognition of scientific, religious, philosophical views.) Who do faiths say that I am? What is man? One God or none? What is religion? The on-going quest. (This could provide a place to include the Bahai faith, Jehovah's Witnesses and others, and new Hindu or Christian movements and Maoism.)

Growth is not arbitrary. Sometimes, as at the moment of birth, there is a suddenness and shock, but more often year flows into year, a birthday may mean new birth, though a change of school or class may be more important. The stages outlined above are intended to flow into one another. Their value lies in stating that there is a progression

and suggesting that each stage is important. They are guide-lines for
the teacher. In planning a scheme of work it is suggested that he
should have his children in mind, and then his material, and that he
should ask himself how far, at that given time, he can take the
majority of the class or a given group. He may decide to describe the
deliberation with which a Muslim prepares for prayer, showing
children the compass, the prayer carpet, and slides showing the
ablutions and prayer positions. He may also make use of records of
the call to prayer. For the moment that might well be sufficient. His
aim is to describe, making the practice of prayer as realistic as
possible. Having accomplished this, however, some child may wish to
go further, or the class as a whole may push him on. Why do Muslims
wash before saying their prayers? What if they're in the desert? Why
do they use a carpet? Why the prayer positions? Why Arabic? What
does a Muslim think about as he stands in the prayer line behind the
Imam? Being pushed about like this is a mark of success, and it is
quite proper when the pressure is coming from the class. Let them
progress as far as they can, not as far as the teacher predetermines.
But what if someone asks which is the right way to pray, or which God
is the real one—'ours' or 'theirs'? Is the class as a whole ready to
discuss these issues? The first question is not too difficult. Islam like
other religions teaches that the attitude of heart and mind matters
more than posture. This might be dealt with in class. The other
question is a matter for a private chat between the individual and the
teacher with the aim of trying to help the pupil think through some of
the issues involved; and let us remember that it is easy to ask Stage 5
questions long before the capacity exists for understanding their
implications or the answers to them.

AN EXAMPLE OF PROGRESSION

Without intending to be controversial, but trying to be helpful,
perhaps I can try to handle the teaching aspects of the sharpest thorn
of all: Christmas.

The first approach would be through what happens at Christmas
within the child's experience. Decorations, the tree, presents, Father
Christmas, cards, food and drink, joy. This is the folk religion to be
accepted rather than analysed, criticised or even supplemented by the
Christmas story. However, although in Tibet we might get away with
saying it's Jesus' birthday and for Christians he is such an important
person that they celebrate it in the manner described, we can't really
hope to find such virgin soil in England outside a few reception centres
in Bradford and elsewhere. We are therefore driven beyond this to
Stage 2, though we shouldn't pass it by. We may have to tell selected

parts of the narratives—not wicked Herod or the angels, I suggest, but first of all the stories behind the Christmas tree, the plum pudding and Santa Claus. Eventually Christmas in other lands or at other times.

At Stage 3 we come to the significance of Christmas for Christians. That it is a joyous and important time would have been realised already, but now perhaps is the time to look at the narratives, perhaps by comparing some Christmas cards with the descriptions given by Matthew and Luke. What do the cards highlight? Choirs of angels, a rough stable, a child with a halo, kings kneeling before a baby. What do these episodes say to Christians at a devotional level?

At the fourth stage we definitely come to the narratives in their totality. The Annunciation, the attitude of Herod, the Virgin Birth, the Nunc Dimittis and Magnificat, and the theology behind them all and behind the story of John the Baptist leaping in Elizabeth's womb. We are passing quickly from the stories to the theology they declare and also from the person of Jesus to his work, which the birth narratives clearly introduce.

Finally, what does the Nativity and Incarnation state about the Christian concept of God? 'Soteriology', 'Christology', 'kenosis' may be words most pupils never hear, but need one be a Barth or a Shankara to understand religion and the issues with which the nativity stories of Jesus, Krishna or Guru Nanak are concerned? This final stage can be theological after the manner of Bunyan's *Pilgrim's Progress* rather than Tillich's *Systematic Theology*! It need not and should not be omitted.

Chapter 6

Bangles, Beads and Fairy Tales: the Use of Ritual Objects outside Their Faith Context

The little statue of Lakshmi which stands on one of my bookshelves is an attractive ornament. It was given to me by a group of third-year students about to leave college and therefore it has additional personal meaning, rather like the now-framed beautiful photograph of the Buddha's footprint which Bury Peerless once sent me as a Christmas card. I now know enough about Hinduism for me to hold this statue of Lakshmi in my hand and call to mind some of the myths which surround her and can even explain some of the iconography. But, even though I may appreciate her left-handedness, being left-handed myself, something is still missing. She is not my deity. She does not evoke a religious response in me. She is an ornament, not an object of devotion. So too with my kirpan and my prayer carpet. Quite a religious museum! But what of the crucifix, what of the Bible or hymn-book as opposed to my eight-volume edition of the Guru Granth Sahib and Pickthall's version of the Qur'an? Here we come up against one of the most important matters in teaching about world religions.

There are two issues really. First, how far should we go in attempting to make my statue of Lakshmi an object of religious devotion in the classroom? Secondly, how are we to make it more than a museum- or aesthetic object? The first question has to do with principle, the second with method.

My own answer to the first question would be not at all. I do not wish to make this statue or a crucifix or the Lord's Prayer something devotional, because that is not my purpose at all in teaching RE in a maintained school. On the other hand, for those to whom these things or words are sacred I hope I shall provide some support and assurance. It is far from my desire to undermine faith where it exists. Turning to the second question, it seems important that as far as possible students should appreciate the religious significance which ritual objects or words have for those who stand within the particular faith. For me the words of institution in the Communion service are more than history; they have taken me to the Last Supper. It seems proper that pupils should know what these words can mean to a

Christian, what the Mool Mantra can mean to a Sikh or the Shema to a Jew. If this view is accepted, how is the significance to be conveyed?

The words or ritual objects might be put into their liturgical context using tapes, slides or films if possible, so that the students may see and hear how they fit into worship. They will learn not only how the object is used, but also the attitude which the devotee has towards it. This comes to life especially when, for example, a scroll is carried in procession during synagogue worship. The significance of the Torah is manifested in the reactions of the congregation.

The place of the subject of the study in this whole tradition needs to be considered, the Shema in the context of the Torah as a whole, the Torah pointer or the Sikh chauri in the context of reverence for the sacred book.

Words might be given greater importance by being heard in the original language and seen in the Hebrew or Arabic script. Listening to the famous recording of a Russian choir singing the Creed, or hearing someone read the Lord's Prayer in French or German, can also be a means of prefacing the study of the all-too-familiar.

The Lord's Prayer is an example of a saying which has a story attached to it. The followers of Jesus asked him to teach them how to pray. This context is important as well as the contemporary liturgical one.

With regard to statues and pictures aesthetic considerations can be important. Bad art is no better for being a plastic statue of the Virgin Mary or a painting of Krishna, but here we are confronted by another problem which the teacher must finally resolve for himself. There are paintings of Indian deities and holy men such as Tulsi Das, Gandhi or Sai Baba. They are rather garish to the Western eye and have little artistic merit. However, they are authentic. They are to be found in temples in England and are on sale in all parts of India and adorn the walls of many homes. English children seem more able to cope with them than adults can. Perhaps it is because the idiom and the subject are both strange. It seems to be the familiar, Christian, so-called art which arouses their indignation. Personally, therefore, I have no hesitation about using the Indian religious pictures. I am far more concerned about the impact which VCOAD or OXFAM black-and-white photographs of India have upon pupils. Even those which show ploughing or folk-dance as opposed to poverty seem depressive, and certainly lack the colour and brightness which is part of the Indian scene no matter how ugly or poor it may be.

In using statues or pictures the teacher is likely to encounter a difficulty which does not exist in the same form when using words. The English, Welsh or Scots, as a whole, belong to a tradition which despises and dislikes devotional objects. Perhaps most RE teachers do, and some of the older ones have not been mellowed by the ecumenical movement. They may feel uncomfortable when they are teaching about Hindu puja or examining Roman Catholic worship. Together with their pupils they have to learn that education is not a matter of expressing opinions and making instant judgements and evaluations, but has to do with learning and understanding. We all have prejudices—they are to be coped with, not exhibited in the classroom! The object of the exercise is to discover what puja or the Mass means to a Hindu or a Roman Catholic, not what they mean to me or to Jones minor, who regards all religion as rubbish anyway.

Words present their own pitfalls. First, there are the names of objects. For example, let us consider three. First the Sikh Kara, worn round the right wrist. Sometimes this is called a bangle and sometimes teachers have forbidden children to wear it in school, classing it as a piece of jewellery. The word 'kara' is used of the iron hoop which holds a wooden bucket or barrel together. The kara symbolises union with God, and the word 'bangle' or 'bracelet' is therefore completely misleading. Sometimes the Sikh chauri waved over the Guru Granth Sahib is called a 'fly-flicker' or 'fly-whisk', even by Sikhs, and again the symbolism of authority is lost in regarding it as merely functional and rather quaint, especially in an English gurdwara in December! The third example is the tasbir of ninety-nine beads which Muslims sometimes use in their devotions. Once I saw a picture of President Sadat sitting with his tasbir. The caption below it read: 'President Sadat with his worry beads.' No prizes are awarded for guessing the monthly in which it appeared! The use of language is important. 'Prayer carpet' sounds much better than 'prayer mat', and 'unburnt brick' much better than 'mud' when describing the fabric of a village house. When did we last describe Anne Hathaway's cottage as a mud hut?

The use of theological language demands no less care. We often forget that our subject has its own technical vocabulary and that its proper usage differs considerably from its use in everyday language. This vocabulary has to be taught. The classic example is the word 'myth', a perfectly respectable religious term but one so much damaged that I have known it upset a Jewish rabbi, who denied that the creation stories of Genesis were myths, and Christian congregations when applied to the Nativity stories. There are others. 'Christian' in everyday parlance means a kind man and nothing more. When I have asked my mature students to define the word 'Christianity' I have received a variety of interesting answers, most of which have more to do with morals than beliefs. Moving from the general area to the particular world-religions situation, we must be on our guard when words like 'sin' and 'salvation' are used. Sometimes Hindus and Sikhs mean something similar to Christians when they use the word 'sin', but more often they mean pollution. 'Incarnation' is another such term. Hindus may use it to translate the term 'avatar', but there is a world of difference between the Hindu and Christian concepts.

For safety's sake we must learn to adopt the terms of the faith we are studying—'kara', 'tasbir', 'avatar', 'moksha', even 'Allah' and 'Brahman' for the word meaning God bring different ideas to mind for Jew, Christian, Muslim, Hindu and Sikh. I have heard well-intentioned Muslims misrepresenting their faith by expressing it in Christian language too often for me to be satisfied with less. Into this category I put also 'mosque', 'synagogue' and 'gurdwara', of course; to call them 'churches' is completely inadequate.

The place of the Bible in RE has been hotly debated in recent years. There is sometimes a tendency on the part of those who would use it very cautiously to be less rigorous with regard to stories of Guru Nanak, the Buddha or Krishna. It seems advisable to remember that a myth divorced from its belief context can become nothing more than a fairy tale. It ceases to be evocative and powerful; it is merely odd or, if told well, interesting. Judaeo-Christian myths are often more likely to receive a sympathetic response from Hindu or Sikh children than from English children of a vestigial Christian culture. They belong to a society which, for too long, has subjected religious narratives to 'scientific method' and has thus lost the skill of appreciating the significance of a story, whether it is to be regarded as historically factual or not. For many such children the Christmas stories are no more meaningful and evocative than those of the child Krishna.

One or two vexed questions remain even when proper attitudes are adopted to ritual objects, language and the scriptures and they are put into their own context and understood in their own idiom. The Quaker in his simple meeting for worship is saying something about ritual and sacramental worship. Somewhere in a study of Christian worship the tensions must emerge. Where?

Jesus, to take the most notable example, is a person of contention. The Muslim respects him highly as a prophet. No true Muslim should speak ill of him, but the Qur'anic revelation denies the divinity of Jesus. The very title Christ, we might remember, is anathema to the Jew when applied to Jesus. Some Jews may nowadays respect Jesus, but he is more properly to be regarded as one who led the people astray. Somewhere the different assessments of Jesus must come out. Where?

In the last paragraph the phrase 'Qur'anic revelation' was used. Is the Qur'an the word of God? Is it revelation? Is the Guru Granth Sahib revelation? Fundamental issues can emerge from the study of world religions. Should they?

Here, again, is an issue of principle which the teacher must eventually decide according to his own lights. Some teachers in universities, schools and colleges stop short of attempting to tackle ultimate questions. They teach about Hinduism or Buddhism. They do not feel it necessary to make one religion confront another or to ask students to grapple with the sort of issues raised in the last few paragraphs. The faiths are studied in parallel, with no converging. Other teachers feel the need to round the study of religion off by facing them, and the study of ultimate questions provides an apex. The one word of guidance which I would offer is to say that description must come before the discussion of other matters. The student must understand the Muslim concept of the unity of God and Jewish beliefs about the Messiah before he can examine Muslim or Jewish attitudes to Jesus. He must understand Muslim and Jewish beliefs about the Qur'an and the Torah; only then is he ready to consider ultimate questions about revelation. If they are reached at all, it must be when the student knows what it means to be a Jew or a Muslim or a Christian in terms of belief and practice. He must be at the conclusion of the syllabus. If the pupils be asked the question 'Are any of them true?', to put it crudely, it should be after the distinctiveness of some of them has been studied, not before. The fact that no criteria exist for answering the question other than those of personal faith is one reason why some teachers discourage the discussion of it. It may be more advisable academically to stop at the various attitudes to Jesus, discussions on the essence of worship, the meaning of the word 'God', and the way in which those who believe in God and those who do not make sense of life. However, pupils whose interest has been aroused are unlikely to halt when teacher blows the whistle. Shouldn't this be seen as the penalty of successful teaching?

Chapter 7

A Thematic Approach to Teaching World Religions

The rapid growth of teaching world religions in schools is not merely an attempt to provide a social therapy in a changing civilisation. It reflects a general movement in which curricula are seen

(1) in a world rather than a parochial context;
(2) in terms of some integration (or, at least, extended subjects in which the subject itself is itself seen to be an integrated study) rather than restricted and isolated subjects;
(3) as social problem-seeing—problem-solving studies rather than being primarily concerned with the acquisition of knowledge;
(4) as forms of episodic concentric rather than sequential studies.

More important, however, world religions has become a central element in attempts to redefine the nature of the subject. Instead of seeing RE as a means of initiating pupils into Christianity, it represents a desire to sensitise pupils to the religious dimension of man and its far-reaching influences. This means that pupils ought to have the opportunity to achieve such fundamental aims as those shown in Table 1.

The problem of devising strategies which might render them attainable inevitably reveals the divisions which exist among RE teachers. It is too easy, on the one hand, to consider RE in splendid purity and isolation and, on the other, as a low-status subject whose content can be mixed and twisted at will to contribute towards the social education of pupils. Both extremes are obviously wrong. Clearly one must recognise that it is part of the total curriculum—a fact which imposes

Table 1   *Some Aims for Religious Education*

The pupils should:
(1) have the opportunity to explore and understand the conceptual framework, rationality and structure of religion;
(2) be shown how the religious dimension has influenced human experience both for good and bad;
(3) recognise the significance which commitment to a religious faith has in the establishment of life-perspectives and how this has influenced motivation, priorities, social order, etc.;

(4) be offered the opportunity to explore the quality, values and dynamic of religious thought as manifested in the world's religious heritage— even if it is unlikely that pupils will appreciate the wealth, beauty and creative power within the faiths;

(5) relearn their culture, bearing in mind pupils may come from Christian or non-Christian backgrounds;

(6) be educated for mutual respect and awareness, bearing in mind that rationality is relative to the parent culture and is largely socially determined;

(7) be helped in their moral education, although one must remember that morality is only one constituent part of religion and not its sum-total;

(8) develop such religious skills as:

    (*a*) the ability to interpret technical jargon
    (*b*) the ability to interpret religious symbolism
    (*c*) understanding the religious interpretation of issues
    (*d*) an awareness of religious phenomena and their significance
    (*e*) enough knowledge to be able to give a 'religious' answer to a problem.

Table 2   *Strengths and Weaknesses of a Thematic Approach*

Strengths	*Weaknesses*
(1) Themes can be modified to highlight aims and objectives.	(1) Faiths (or any other topic) are distorted because no faith is like the range of fragments which will be used in different themes. (But isn't all learning a distortion of reality?)
(2) Key ideas can be highlighted with minimum distractions.	
(3) Religious ideas can be brought back into focus to give reinforcement and a clear conceptual framework.	(2) Simplistic stereotypes may be established.
(4) Themes can draw upon an exceptionally wide range of content for fresh material and branching studies.	(3) The realisation of the significance of the links between the religion and the culture might be minimal, and the problems of holding cultural differences in mind are enormous.

(5) Their flexibility enables:
  (*a*) a wide range of teaching strategies to be developed;
  (*b*) themes to be developed or concluded as required;
  (*c*) a wide range of interests to be satisfied. All of these increase the possibility of achieving child-centred studies.
	(4) The pupils may end up with a rag-bag of knowledge which contains no worthwhile form unless they are aware of an over-all structure of religion.

(6) Their versatility enables teachers to draw upon a wide range of resources.	

(7)   The content can be organised to
       develop either a discrete educa-
       tion in religion or to contribute
       to integrated studies.

---

both constraints and opportunities. The challenge is to find ways of using these constraints to some advantage so that one is in a position to capitalise on the educational opportunities, thereby contributing to the pupils' total education.

Although world religions are normally studied systematically in order to convey something of their essential spirit, unique doctrines, internal coherence and human impact, it is probably an illusion to believe that one can enable pupils to capture much of the essential spirit of such faiths as Islam, Judaism, Hinduism and Buddhism because of:

(1)   The cultural barriers. Indeed, one might ask if pupils really understand Christianity and especially that 'foreign' world peopled by Abraham, David, Jesus, Paul, etc.

(2)   The limited range of knowledge and experiental opportunities open to them may confirm the pupils' stereotypes.

(3)   The time factor and RE's juxtaposition with other subjects. If pupils have rushed from PE or mathematics, etc., there may be little possibility of their entering into a meaningful relationship with the faith in question.

(4)   The mere fact that it is part of an institution's programme of instruction militates against fostering a significant degree of sensitivity to the faith being studied, even though pupils are often attracted towards religions other than their own simply because of the differences and freshness. Furthermore, time limits and pupil ability make it doubtful whether more than two religions other than Christianity can be considered, and even then it is difficult to decide when they can be introduced with any reasonable hope of success. But perhaps, even if this is done well, it cannot give an adequate picture of contemporary world religions.

The question here is whether a thematic approach to world religions is a viable strategy which is efficient and flexible enough to meet the demands for religious integrity and also the needs of the pupils and schools. The basic advantages and problems are clear (see Table 2).

Whilst the wide range of organisational variables and constraints which can virtually dominate the practical teaching situation makes the characteristic flexibility and versatility of thematic strategies very attractive, this in itself should not unduly sway curriculum decision-makers in their judgements. Instead they should explore the question of whether it offers a rich and varied basis for content selection which can help pupils to develop a coherent understanding of mankind's diverse concepts of God, self and community.

Whilst not suggesting that it should be *the* strategy for teaching world religions, it will be argued that it can profitably and conveniently slot in with other approaches within the context of both the discrete subject of RE and the humanities, and so make the aims mentioned earlier attainable.

WITHIN THE CONTEXT OF THE DISCRETE SUBJECT

Many criteria for curriculum selection used by teachers of religion are common to all teachers—namely, the pursuit of truth, coherence, skills and clarity, explaining and revealing the dynamism of human conduct, meeting the needs of pupils and provoking a new and wider sense of awareness. Further, they too want to ensure that any resultant curriculum contains a steady flow of fresh knowledge which increases the complexity of the over-arching concepts which are integral to it.

Religion, however, has unique characteristics which must be developed if it is to retain its integrity, and the following five distinct types of thematic work show how this may be achieved.

(*a*) basic conceptual themes
(*b*) themes related to particular religions
(*c*) inter-actionist themes
(*d*) themes which explore common elements in religious life
(*e*) societal and moral themes.

Basic Conceptual Themes
All religions share certain basic concepts, even though their manifestations and interpretations differ considerably. Therefore, it might be reasonable to establish with, say, 11-year-olds a clear conceptual framework of religion's essential elements. This foundation will not only ensure that pupils will have some resource material and concepts upon which to draw when they study world religions (including Christianity) systematically, but will also help to resolve other problems.

Key elements or concepts have formed the basis of man's religious experience and expression. These may be analysed into the following themes:

(*a*) mystery and inquiry
(*b*) (i) the religious interpretation of nature and the universe

(ii) inquiry into creation to find life's creator(s) and sustainer(s)
(c) the religious interpretation given to human life-patterns (e.g., birth, marriage and death)
(d) worship (its objects, places and forms), faith and prayer
(e) good and evil
(f) life and death
(g) sacrifice and its mediatorial function
(h) holy men
(i) holy books
(j) communications—signs and symbols
(k) revelation and authority
(l) conflict and harmony, decline and reform.

These powerful and dominant conceptual themes not only lay the foundation for an understanding of world religions, but they also readily allow the doctrinal, mythological, ethical, ritualistic, experimental and sociological elements (N. Smart) to be introduced and then later developed repeatedly in different contexts through concentric studies, thereby giving the pupils some notion of the structure of religious thought within different religions.

In subsequent years these dominant themes can become *recurring secondary themes* so that as the whole course proceeds the pupils not only gain a firm grasp of the essential nature of religion, but also have a store of knowledge upon which to draw when studying various world religions. It also obviates the common charge that thematic work lacks coherence and continuity.

It can be argued that such a teacher-centred conceptual approach might be 'dry' and not sufficiently child-orientated. This is not necessarily true because the religious concepts can be given life if they are explored and developed against the backcloth of the world-wide human experience at both the personal and societal levels. Furthermore, this will emphasise that, important though the dominant religious concepts are, religion is primarily concerned with commitment and the effects of allegiance.

This thematic conceptual approach might be developed in two ways—that is, either by illustrating the key concepts from within one particular society or by showing each concept in relation to a range of different societies. It is crucial to stress, however, that it is not permissible to make straight comparisons between different religions and the religious beliefs of social groups because of the wide range of cultural variables, but one can note the underlying similarities.

These two approaches might be illustrated through the concepts of sacrifice. In different forms, sacrifices have been offered for four main reasons—for thank-offering, forgiveness, intercession (e.g., health, victory, etc.) and communion (i.e., sharing the divine power), and they have invariably been characterised by three elements:

(1) cost and quality
(2) correctness in respect of material and ritual
(3) obedience to certain commandments.

If the concept is developed as a central theme, it may be explored briefly through reference to several religious 'groups' or social tribes (e.g., the Celts, Saxons, Javaros, Incas, Jews, Christianity). Alternatively, one might see the concept and its outworking as being at the heart of one group of people. For example, the temples, priests and sacrificial ceremonies which were at the heart of the Aztec civilisation were of crucial importance in respect of health, food, victory and government.

It is often more convenient to develop this approach initially by studying or referring to societies where religion holds or has held a dominant position (e.g., the Israelites, the Egyptians), because although these foundation concepts can still be seen in modern societies and religions they are often clouded by hosts of other complexities and variables.

This attempt to show man as an interpreter, a 'meaning-maker', a problem-solver and an explorer of the spiritual aspect of life (e.g., creation) may savour of a purely phenomenological interpretation of religion, but it is more than that. At the end of such a foundation course the pupils should not only have an understanding of the essential elements of religion which will provide a frame of reference for any future study of world religions, but also have positive expectations for the future in religious education.

It is important to remember that, when themes are being developed through concentric studies, the over-arching *ideas* and *concepts* must recur within the context of fresh knowledge if they are not to pall. If the *body* of *knowledge* is tightly restricted and developed in a concentric pattern as in some old agreed syllabuses, it is very difficult to prevent the pupils thinking that they know it already. This is significant because, although the teacher is primarily concerned with the acquisition, consolidation and development of the fundamental concepts of religion, the children are usually knowledge- and progress-orientated and hold the old knowledge which they first met years previously in low esteem and as 'kids' stuff'. The teacher's resultant problems are enormous, because pupils react according to their expectations and often are not receptive to the development of old knowledge as opposed to old ideas 'dressed' in fresh knowledge. Unless pupils, who may not share the teacher's value judgements about such important content, meet an invigorating flow of fresh knowledge, they may be excused for summarily dismissing it without too much serious thought—especially if they have been socialised into a powerful, lusty cynicism. An even graver danger is that by dismissing religion with that particular content they may deprive themselves of a basic form of human understanding.

By breaking free from traditional constraints, not only are esteem and expectancy heightened, but also religion is given an authority and freshness when children see it as a world-wide historical/contemporary phenomenon rather than merely a 'quirk' of Christians, Jews, Muslims, etc., and that in fact religion has been the *norm* which has helped to satisfy and give direction to social, psychological and spiritual needs and aspirations.

Themes Related to Particular Religions

Once the basic concepts of religion have been taught, the teacher may well consider how a thematic strategy might be applied to teaching about *particular* religions. This might be approached by identifying themes which show religion and religions in their historical/developmental context and which also show the basis of their religious and moral teaching.

There is no completely satisfactory way of implementing this policy fairly and fully, because even if both teacher and pupils focus their attention on the essential character of a religion one is forced to ask how long can be spent on it. Can it be more than one term of, say, twenty-four lessons? Will this enable a teacher when examining Islam to give the pupils a clear understanding of Muhammad and his personal faith, to realise the extent of the impact of Islam, to appreciate the basic tenets of the faith and their implications for Muslims? It must be questionable, especially if two or three religions are considered in turn with only a minimal referral to them in subsequent lessons. Most Christian teachers would be worried if Christianity were so treated, and Muslims or Humanists must be expected to have precisely the same concern to the same degree.

Perhaps it is more realistic to study the religions through six concentric themes: founders and their disciples, the characteristics (e.g., customs, festivals, etc.), growth, impact, creative and insightful genius, and the religious teaching of the faith concerned. Although it may be difficult to accept that each religion will not be taught as one 'seamless whole', it will enable teachers constantly to refer back to previous studies in each religion and so ensure that the pupils' new knowledge is not forgotten quickly. Perhaps one question facing teachers is whether discrete faiths should be studied through themes or whether themes should be developed through reference to specific faiths.

Of course, one is not trying to compare and evaluate religious systems, but rather to look for similarities and differences in the attitudes of adherents in respect of basic theology, commitment, life-styles and the influence of different forms of religious heritage.

Inter-actionist Themes

The place of the major religions or any indigenous faith in such a thematic course must be considered carefully in view of its profound influence on the development of the parent culture, not to mention the fact that a teacher's personal commitment usually makes it difficult to regard Christianity as simply another world religion.

Any coherent course based on the theme of the development and expansion of Christianity as a world religion (e.g., Jesus, Paul and his missionary journeys, Christianity's arrival in Britain or elsewhere in Europe, and the missionary impulse which took it to India, China, etc.) will naturally introduce other key religions at the point where they inter-act with Christianity. In addition, it is advisable to pro-gramme into the course topics which indicate foci of common religious expression or conflict.

The contemporary inter-actionist approach normally focuses on the areas of inter-action between the faiths of Christian, Hindu, Muslim and Sikh immigrants with the British population and churches, or by examining places such as Nigeria and Java where different religions co-exist. Although this might seem to be a 'real' and perfect solution, it does raise the problem of prejudice.

It is usually both efficient and convenient to study the inter-acting religions through four themes such as:

(1) the influence of the religions on their followers;
(2) the influence of the religions on surrounding communities and social life;
(3) problems facing the minority religion;
(4) conflict, co-operation and co-existence between the religions.

Themes Which Explore Common Elements in Religious Life

It is often useful to break up the approach which shows religions in their historical context by interposing within it thematic projects such as holy books, creativity, mythology and religious symbolism.

Two effective ways of dealing with such themes, if they are not to extend into the humanities, is either to select topics which form the heart of the theme and illustrate these from religions as appropriate, or else to focus the theme on various religions in turn. For example:

(1*a*) *Holy Books*
  (i) The magic and authority of holy books
  (ii) Books for worship and praise
  (iii) Books for doctrine and teaching
  (iv) Books for history
  (v) Books to be fought for

(1*b*)
  (i) The function of religious books
  (ii) The Qur'an (impact, teaching and worship)
  (iii) The Bible (impact, teaching and worship)
  (iv) The Talmud (impact, teaching and worship)
  (v) The Vedas (impact, teaching and worship)

(2*a*) *Creativity and Beauty*
  (i) Buildings
  (ii) Art
  (iii) Dance
  (iv) Music and song
  (v) The written word

(2*b*)
  (i) The geneii of religious creativity
  (ii) Creativity in 'primitive' religions
  (iii) Creativity in Islam
  (iv) Creativity in Hinduism
  (v) Creativity in Christianity

(3*a*) *Myth*
  (i) What myths are
  (ii) Myths of creation and origins
  (iii) Myths which help problem-solving (e.g., illness and drought)
  (iv) Myths as the basis of social life
  (v) Myths in worship

(3*b*)
  (i) Myths to give certainty or confidence
  (ii) Myths in primitive societies
  (iii) Myths in Islam
  (iv) Myths in Hinduism
  (v) Myths in Christianity

(4*a*) *Symbolism*
  (i) Symbolism at the heart of religion
  (ii) Symbolism in movement
  (iii) Symbolism through sound
  (iv) Symbolism through art and design
  (v) Symbolism in literature

(4*b*)
  (i) Symbolism through sound and sight aid worship and identity
  (ii) Symbolism in primitive religions
  (iii) Symbolism in Islam
  (iv) Symbolism in Hinduism
  (v) Symbolism in Christianity

In practice one usually uses the topics in each of the *a*-type thematic developments as microtopics for studying *b*-type topic components.

No matter which approach one uses it is suggested here that the key concepts (see pp. 65-6) should be programmed into the themes so that they not only recur but also develop from a concrete to a more sophisticated level of understanding. For example, the concept of sacrifice would gradually develop from the sacrifice of animals to self-sacrificial service in everyday life.

Societal and Moral Themes

One should be able to assume that after studies such as the ones outlined pupils will understand the fundamental concepts in world religions and also know how religions have developed and what characterises them. Therefore, the pupils should be ready to examine religions in their social context.

This not only roughly coincides with the normal interests associated with the adolescent's social and moral development, but also shows religion's relevance to everyday life. For example, one might consider the effect of religion on government, food, warfare, health, human rights, and justice.

Any consideration of such themes would need to show:

(*a*) How religious beliefs have dominated life-styles in societies and religions.
(*b*) How religious beliefs are moving from a position of control to one of influence.
(*c*) How these themes influence people in contemporary society.

These themes might be developed as follows:

Theme		*Stage A sub-topics*		*Stage B sub-topics*
(1) Food	(*a*)	Food as symbols in religion, expressing joy, sealing vows	(*a*)	Religion and food—causing and preventing problems
	(*b*)	Practices to acknowledge God the provider	(*b*)	Religion helps in the problem
	(*c*)	Food as a symbol in Islam	(*c*)	Religious pressure-groups
	(*d*)	Food as a symbol in Hinduism	(*d*)	Jewish food practices
	(*e*)	Food as a symbol in Christianity (e.g., Eucharist, Lent, etc.)	(*e*)	The individual's response to the situation
(2) Health	(*a*)	Health, pain and goodness — a religious interpretation	(*a*)	Health in nature and religion
	(*b*)	Healing customs in India	(*b*)	Health as a challenge to faith
	(*c*)	Health amongst Jews or Muslims	(*c*)	Drinks, drugs and religious responses
	(*d*)	Jesus the healer	(*d*)	Faith and medical healing

	(e)	Christian healers		(e)	Health and questions of conscience
(3) Warfare	(a)	As a divinely ordered life-style		(a)	Religion during war
	(b)	Holy aids to wars		(b)	Religions at war with each other
	(c)	The warrior gods		(c)	Religions looking for peace (World Council of Churches, World Congress of Faiths, etc.)
	(d)	Religious war		(d)	Christian priests and revolution in South America
	(e)	Spiritual warfare		(e)	Peace and tolerance; Ramakrishna
(4) Government	(a)	Faith governs loyalties—Sikhs		(a)	A plural society in Britain
	(b)	Initiation rites		(b)	Religious pressure-groups on government
	(c)	Religion governing life in Tibet and Japan		(c)	Islam in Pakistan
	(d)	The divine right of kings in Europe		(d)	Faith with and without God— United States and Russia
	(e)	God the King— Islam, Judaism and Christianity		(e)	Morality and political beliefs
(5) Human Rights, Justice	(a)	God the law- and custom-giver		(a)	Religion as a vehicle for good and evil in the modern world
	(b)	Customs to protect family life amongst Sikhs or Muslims		(b)	Religion and civil rights in the United States
	(c)	Justice in Israel		(c)	Religion and political rights; Amnesty International
	(d)	Social rights in Hinduism		(d)	Religion and the right to housing
	(e)	Christianity as protector and persecutor		(e)	Rights for immigrant faiths

The teacher here has the choice of studying the themes in depth—i.e., Topic A followed by Topic B (a strategy particularly suited to CSE courses)—or by developing projects in which the over-arching theme shows the impact of religion on societies where it has been in a dominant position (i.e., Topics A in the above example), followed by a series of projects in which pupils study the same themes in a modern setting where religion is an influential (i.e., Topics B) rather than a dominant force.

This approach once again illustrates the flexibility of a thematic approach towards world religions.

Within the Context of the Humanities
The emergence of the humanities has been accelerated by a redefinition of the curriculum in many schools which has cumulatively had far-reaching consequences. The humanities, along with the other forms of integrated studies, such as social studies, environmental studies, liberal studies, the creative arts, and environmental sciences, characterise a new 'atmosphere' in schools and offer new opportunities and pose new problems for their integral subjects, but none more so than for RE within the humanities. Bearing in mind that this, as with so many curriculum developments, is based on educated hunches rather than empirical research, it is vital to appraise the situation carefully in order to maximise the alleged benefits and avoid its undoubted dangers.

The underlying assumptions behind every pattern of integration are:

(1) That life itself is a dynamic social and physical arena which transcends any of the disciplines and subjects which are used to study it. Therefore, any single subject can only convey a facet of its drama, colour and essence.
(2) The subjects all contain knowledge, methods of inquiry and means of expression which are complementary to each other when any problem or some other 'life situation' is being studied.
(3) Whilst knowledge cannot be regarded as a 'seamless whole', the grouping of subjects will minimise fragmentation and foster cohesion between study areas or subjects.
(4) The potential flexibility will offer a wider and richer range of teaching and learning experiences, which may thereby meet the needs of and seem relevant to a broad range of pupils. This is especially important as increasing numbers of schools de-stream.

In the humanities, therefore, religion is seen within the total life-style of any community, and should not be totally divorced from the 'geographical' and 'historical' aspects of any study. Further, religion contains conceptual tools which are essential to any balanced study of man.

RE can, of course, satisfactorily contribute to several forms of integrated studies. For example, it can be linked with English in liberal studies, with history in some forms of environmental studies, and with geography and contemporary history in social studies, but a world religions strategy for teaching RE demands that it should be incorporated within the humanities, which is itself a fluid form of organisation, which readily spreads into the fields of social and liberal studies.

If the title 'humanities' is defined as studies which show how man has mastered, used, interpreted, developed and organised his physical and social environment, then both the world of religion and world religions command an important place in education, because the religious dimension has influenced, and still does profoundly influence, man's personal aspirations, moral values and social practices. For example, it is questionable whether purely geographical and historical studies of India, China, South Africa, South America, etc., can be regarded as adequate. A world religions component is essential to help pupils realise not only the influences which are dominant motivating influences, but also how they arrived at decisions which may seem irrational to us in our present society. Similarly there is a distinct danger of any historical study—of, say, the Crusades—degenerating into banal, irrelevant professionalised knowledge if the world religions element is not present.

Looking for Aims and Objectives

Religion is vulnerable within the humanities because it has little apparent utility. Therefore, although in practice many of the aims are either vague or based on organisational imperatives, the aims and objects should be clearly defined, even though one knows that they must be flexible and responsive to the needs of the pupils.

The term 'humanities' normally pre-supposes a considerable degree of integration; but RE teachers, in particular, need to consider the implications of this, because it can result in the religious component being diluted and subsumed into some form of social and moral education, until finally it is dismissed when staffing problems arise. This is especially likely to occur if the integration is contrived and the religious component is expendable. Hence it is possible in a topic such as 'water' to devise a religious contribution which is not essential to the pupils' understanding (e.g., The Flood, Jonah, Jesus walking on the water) and which can be dismissed unless it can be shown to fit into an over-all education in religion. The following outline may be more acceptable.

Water
Over-all theme: The problem it has raised and its uses to man.
History: (*a*)   Water stimulates invention and inquiry.
                (*b*)   Expansion and conquest by water.

Geography: (*a*)   The problem of water supplies in the world, man's inventive genius, and the modern uses of water by man.

              (*b*)   The creation of wealth by water.

RE: (*a*)   Its mystery and life-dependency—a focus for religious inquiry and practice (e.g. rain-dances, etc.)

              (*b*)   Its symbolic value for purity, cleansing and separation.

Therefore, if the religious component does not clearly contribute to an over-all understanding of a distinct facet of man's development, it is possible that when decisions involving priorities are made RE may be seen to be of marginal significance and, therefore, able to be frozen out without too much loss. Teachers of world religions, like teachers of every subject, need to know precisely what contribution their study area makes to the curriculum. Furthermore, before being swept along by a euphoric tide of change, teachers of world religions need to know what knowledge and concepts must be mastered.

What Is Meant by Integration

Once the essential knowledge and concepts have been determined, *then* it is possible to consider what potential areas of legitimate integration exist. This usually takes one of three forms:

(1)   integrated studies where the subjects are subsumed into the topic or theme to such a degree that they lose their identities;

(2)   inter-disciplinary studies;

(3)   co-ordinated studies.

It is usually assumed that integrated studies are more appropriate for younger children. Although this may be true when considering some forms of environmental studies, the term implies that the pupils ought to have 'something' (knowledge, skills and concepts) to integrate. This would suggest, therefore, that RE is more useful in integrated studies amongst older rather than amongst younger pupils.

'Integrated studies' is useful in those humanities faculties where there are courses which have an anthropological/social studies basis. In courses which centre on the changing world of such groups as the Australian aborigines, the eskimoes and the tribes of the Amazon religion can be seen to permeate every aspect of life, which can be explored through drama, art, library assignments, creative writing, etc. In this situation it is often preferable for the teacher of 'the world of religion' to act primarily as a resource adviser.

In secondary schools 'integration' usually takes the form of inter-disciplinary or co-ordinated studies. Whereas in inter-disciplinary studies several subjects may simultaneously focus their knowledge and modes of inquiry on a problem such as hunger or a region such as South Africa, in co-ordinated studies the subjects may be taught with a considerable degree of independence.

In 'co-ordinated studies' curricula, subjects such as religion are taught as distinct entities, so as to enable the subjects' integrity to be maintained and allow the pupils to acquire a sound knowledge of each subject's perspectives, skills and concepts. A degree of cohesion (or integration) is achieved by ensuring that every subject in the humanities explores certain global themes such as man the problem-solver, agricultural man, community life, or exploration and development. 'Bridges' between subjects can be achieved easily if some or all of the subjects choose to centre their work on certain people and regions (e.g., the Vikings or north Africa) and to build into the work the following over-arching concepts which are common to most subjects: inter-action, inter-dependence, cause and effect, authority, marks of civilisation, adaptation, conquest and progress, construction and destruction.

This approach has the added advantages of minimising logistical problems and ensuring some form of continuity.

In co-ordinated studies one does not look for tie-ups between each lesson or group of lessons, because this usually leads to severe distortions, with the subjects being sacrificed to the 'god' of integration. In this case, it is considered that the pupils' knowledge about 'God' and the religious faiths and practices of the world is too important to be bastardised, and that world religions have a form of knowledge which demands a degree of logical development and precludes it from being totally absorbed into integration.

A great deal of genuine integration does exist, however, if the teachers draw together the common principles, ideas and themes at the end of each term or year. The pupils can thus see the underlying coherence and areas of overlap.

If a humanities faculty develops the global themes—

Man Masters and Uses His World
Community Life
Man the Explorer and Developer
Man the Problem-Solver
Man Changes His World

—teachers of world religions can not only adopt all of the strategies suggested in this book, but they can also work with other subjects at the appropriate time without being burdened with further compulsory integration once the section of work is completed.

Teachers of world religions can obviously contribute much to integration within the humanities. It is often overlooked that world religions is a field of integrated study in its own right, naturally moving into music, art, history, geography, etc., but without the necessity of officially using subject specialists. For example, a world religions project on symbolism may take several forms, e.g.:

Type A Illustrate the following from religions as appropriate:
 (i) Symbolism as a means of communication in religions
 (ii) Symbolism in religious art
 (iii) Symbolic sounds and silences in religions
 (iv) Symbolism in religious architecture
 (v) Symbolism in body movements and dress-dance, posture, etc.
 (vi) Symbolism in speech and chants
 (vii) Symbolism in the written word

Type B
A study of the seven components in Type A within one faith.

Type C
A study of the seven components in Type A through one element (e.g., worship) in several faiths.

Whichever approach is adopted, some form of integrated learning takes place.

If the global theme, Man the Problem-Solver, is developed through the sub-topics health, food, human rights, war and peace, government and communications, genuine co-ordination of topic areas and over-arching ideas can be easily achieved with integrity and good will as the following example should indicate.

Health
Who sends disease? The mystery of sickness in Borneo
Spiritual healers and medicine men
Health as a spiritual battle in Taoism, etc.
Health in the Old Testament—its laws and basis of faith—
 also Islam, Buddhism and Hinduism.
Sickness is not due to sin—Jesus
Research into sickness—the Mission to Lepers in India
Can God intervene?—Lourdes, etc.
Wonders of healing in creation—antibodies, etc.
'Man-made' illness—psychiatric disorders, drug addiction, pollution and illness.

Teachers of world religions, therefore, should examine carefully the implications of integration and ensure that it is not a 'mish-mash' of ideas which may be the kiss of death to any meaningful education in world religions.

A Choice of Strategies

Once the aims and objectives have been clarified, and one realises that different definitions of the term 'integration' will result in different types of courses, one must consider the potential which is inherent in the ten following strategies which are employed in schools.

(1) Themes
(2) Topics
(3) Ideas
(4) Regions and systematic studies of religions
(5) A patch approach
(6) Problem-solving
(7) Case-studies
(8) Concentric themes
(9) Social concepts
(10) Skills-led courses

No one strategy is perfect and, therefore, the basic strength of the humanities—its flexibility—should be fully exploited. This may mean exploiting not only different forms of integration, but also several different teaching strategies during each year.

(1) *Themes*
  (a) *Neutral themes*
      Some themes might be regarded as neutral in so far as either every or any cluster of subjects can make a legitimate contribution to an integrated study of the theme or else it can be used as the basis for a subject-centred theme which draws freely upon other subjects as and when required. Examples of these are creativity, survival, conquest, power, protection, war, beauty, urban man, progress, change, boundaries and wealth. This may be developed 'explosively' where each subject explodes the neutral theme into subject-orientated topics which are then exploited semi-independently. For example:

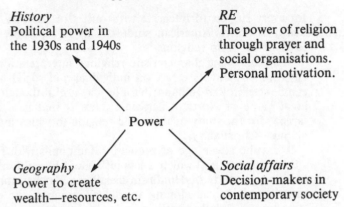

History
Political power in
the 1930s and 1940s

RE
The power of religion
through prayer and
social organisations.
Personal motivation.

Power

Geography
Power to create
wealth—resources, etc.

Social affairs
Decision-makers in
contemporary society

Alternatively the subjects may focus on one aspect of the word (e.g., the power of leaders, or the power of communities), with every subject trying to make a relevant contribution to it. One fascinating theme is boundaries, which focuses on the way in which divisions exist between people, nations, religions, the 'saved' and the privileged/non-privileged.

(b) *Subject themes* In this case, religious themes such as worship, festivals, leaders and disciples, monasticism and myth are common.

(c) *Social themes* These can normally be developed by teachers of every subject in the humanities once the subject foundations have been laid. Examples of this are: government, law, decision-making, courage, caring, immigration, authority.

(2) *Topics*
These are normally much shorter and more specific than themes and involve either integration between two subjects for a few weeks or allowing the subject to be an integrated study. Examples of this are buildings, water, books.

(3) *Ideas*
Within this strategy one normally finds social ideas such as democracy, communism, capitalism, independence, class, etc., which give ample scope for teachers of world religions to contribute to integrated-studies courses with older pupils.

(4) *Regions*
Asian, African and Middle Eastern studies give a humanities department the opportunity to do everything its devotees hope for, especially in the field of world religions. One region, however, which is neglected but which offers a superb opportunity

for every subject to integrate with others or to work independently is North American studies. This is especially true for teachers of world religions.

Many different characteristic religious interpretations of the environment and its effect on individual and social behaviour can be seen in Red Indian tribal life but, useful though it is, the great value of North American studies is that it is a superb 'arena' for the study of the world religion to which many of us belong—Christianity.

It has the advantage of presenting the pupils with fresh and stimulating material which is less influenced by cultural barriers than, say, a study of Hinduism usually is. Furthermore, it is a superb study for developing an understanding of the concepts, structures and skills of religion.

Not only is the proverbial diversity stimulating, but it also shows how religious faith and organised religion can govern or influence individual and corporate life in politics, business and every other facet of social life. It also shows how a fragmented religion might respond to a problem-solving situation in a pluralistic society. Such diversity exists that one might make a comparative study of religion within a religion because all of the characteristics of religion are present in many different conflicting or competing forms. Where else in contemporary society can one see such fast-moving developments to show the impact of religion on national aspirations and practices? With the presence of minority groups of every persuasion, there is no shortage of material for the teacher of world religions! The following brief outline will give some idea of the scope of the contribution of world religions to North American studies.

Topic	*Ideas to be covered*
(1) Before the White Man	Religious interpretations of the environment and their impact on tribal life.
(2) Conquest and the Spanish Catholics	Mission and divine conquest through the alliance of church and state. A study of the Franciscans, Dominicans.
(3) The New France	The work of Jesuits with settlers and Indians.
(4) English Settlers	Puritans in Plymouth, Boston, Anglicans in Jamestown.
(5) Holy Experiments	Winthrop, Penn, etc.—attempts at Christian government.
(6) The Great Awakening	The phenomenon of the decline-

		revival cycle as seen in the work of Jonathan Edwards. The churches as pressures for change.
(7)	The War of Independence	The question of a state church or not.
(8)	Gone West	The Frontier—the responses to the challenge—the belief in independence.
(9)	Missionary Problems	Opportunist churches in the nineteenth century.
(10)	A City for the Saints	Mormons.
(11)	Slavery	Human rights and various religious interpretations. The limited changes brought about by the white church.
(12)	A Place of Our Own	The impact of immigrants on churches and strains on religious allegiance.
(13)	Demon Rum	The impact of a minority church on government—prohibition laws.
(14)	The Depression	The social gospel of the 1920s and 1930s.
(15)	Civil Rights	The churches as pressures for change face rivals in the Black Power movement.
(16)	Protest against War	The American sense of mission and the influence of churches as part of the nation's conscience.
(17)	Government	The impact of Christianity on government policies—Christianity and capitalism.
(18)	Bible Battles	The conflict between religion and science and between old and new attitudes to the Bible.
(19)	Missions Overseas	Types of missionary activity and a reappraisal of missions.
(20)	The Wind, the Fire and the Spirit	New movements spreading through the Church—Jesus People, Charismatic movement.

Other regions such as Russia and China also provide excellent opportunities to show the different faces of religion in a challenging age of change.

(5) *Patch approach*

This well-established strategy focuses on one place or period and is often led by history or geography with world religions acting in a servicing capacity. Such 'patches' as a modern Egyptian town, a Viking village and Florence are examples suited to this approach.

(6) *Problem-solving*
     This typical inter-disciplinary form of study is frequently used to
     study such problems as hunger, peace, equality, wealth and
     human rights with appropriate religious content being drawn
     from many religions as appropriate. This may be developed
     through a case-study strategy (see 7) as follows:

     Hunger in India
     Historical, geographical and religious reasons for hunger
     Religious food-laws and their impact
     Agencies for the alleviation of hunger and their motives
     Working with the Indian Government
     Farm re-organising and agricultural education
     Indian anger against missions and some relief agencies

(7) *Case-studies*
     These usually relate to a person or an incident and try to look for
     the motives which provoked the main actions considered in the
     case-study. The 'hero'-type case-study (e.g., Theresa of Calcutta)
     is a convenient spotlight for religious motivation and practice
     which can lead to a natural divergence into other faiths.
         Case-studies about immigrant families are also fertile areas for
     teachers of world religions, especially as they are sufficiently
     detailed to allow the pupils to identify with the joys and problems
     of the families.

(8) *Concentric themes*
     This interesting strategy is ideal when trying to combine subject-
     teaching with integrated studies in the early years of secondary
     school. When studying social groups or the foundations of
     civilisations, RE teachers are faced with the dilemma of main-
     taining a cohesion within their subject and yet also making an
     appropriate contribution to the integrated study. This can be
     resolved by selecting, say, five key concepts in religion and
     developing these through each different integrated study in turn
     as the following outline indicates:

		Worship Sacrifice Creation Holy men, Signs and symbols etc.
Hunters	Bushmen	
and	Eskimoes	
Warriors	Red Indians	
	Australian Aborigines	
Pastoral	Ashanti	
and	Masai	
Agricultural	Red Indians	
	Sherpas	

Early European	Celts
	Vikings
	Central Europeans
	Greeks/Romans
Ancient Middle East	The Nile
	Tigris-Euphrates
	Persia
	Canaan
Central and South America	Mayas
	Aztecs
	Incas
	Haiti
Seafarers	Polynesia
	Equador
	Philippines

(9) *Recurring social concepts*

If the humanities is trying to show what is human about man, and how and why he inter-acts with society, teachers can profitably use the following concepts which permeate human society as a basis for history, geography and RE courses.

(1) Control and Freedom
Power
Patterns of government
Succession
The Law

(2) Allegiance and Rivalry
Family, tribe and nation
Social support systems to promote allegiance—myths, legends, customs
Moral codes

(3) Dominance and Submission
Aspiration
Exploitation
Expansion
Submission

(4) Progress and regression
Invention
Resources and their uses
Impact of technology
Interdependence

(5) Phenomenal/environmental basis of historical development
(a) land
(b) sea
(c) availability of resources

(6) Aesthetic and spiritual
Art
Music
Architecture
Religion (aspects of)

These would act as guides and terms of reference rather than determinants of content. Furthermore, even if the content between subjects differs, there will still be an appreciable degree of integration and teachers of world religions will have relative freedom in the choice of curriculum content.

(10) *Skills-led courses*

This is the most controversial strategy, because it is suggesting that the choice, teaching and learning of specialist 'content' is of secondary importance to the acquisition of skills. There are four groups of skills:

social	basic learning skills
higher inquiry	specialist subject

Of these, only the last gives pre-eminence to content, whereas the others stress that integration can occur through the processes involved in the learning experiences. Although the choice of topics may be of secondary importance, skills must be taught and learned through some content, and teachers of world religions may well find that a 'skills' strategy gives them great freedom of choice in the selection of content.

Clearly the humanities can be taught through specialist subject and integrated studies approaches. Teachers of world religions can contribute to both these ranges of strategies. However, two pertinent questions are raised:

How long can any strategy be sustained?

Is it possible to fit the strategies into a developmental pattern?

Conclusion

It should be apparent that a thematic approach is neither 'the answer' nor 'the *bête noir*' when teaching world religions, but it should form a key part of the total strategy because:

(1) it can be used to teach the basic concepts of religion and give a clear understanding of the religious rationality which stems from commitment to faith and some degree of sensitivity for religious motives which influence actions, choices and decisions.

(2) it is capable of variety and so meeting the changing opportunities and the diverse interests and demands of the pupils and the profession.

(3) it can foster the order and coherence which are necessary to give a sense of progression and completion.

(4) it is flexible enough to meet the changing requirements of the pupils, the subject and the school at this time of experimentation.

These qualities should prevent this facet of inquiry, wisdom, expression and energy being debased in the pupils' eyes and achieve some degree of understanding of religious ideas and practices and the inter-relatedness between religious thought, structures, concepts and skills in 'total life' contexts.

Chapter 8

World Religions in the Multi-Faith School

It might appear obvious that a number of religions should be taught in schools where there are Muslim and Jewish children as well as pupils from many Christian denominations—in such schools the latter are frequently from East Europe and the Caribbean. However, in such places one very often encounters Bible-based, moralistic teaching or no religious education at all, accompanied by either of two state-ments, 'If they've come here they need to know about our religion,' or 'We don't want to upset anyone, so we treat them all alike and avoid mentioning differences—like religion.' Both assertions are half-true and should not be ignored, though the real reasons for not teaching about Islam in a school with Muslim pupils in it is much more compli-cated and worthy of someone's careful analytical research.

A host of multi-racial schools are now multi-faith in the real sense that the various religions present are recognised both in the classroom and in assembly. There is a growing literature on the subject but, above all, advisers, often themselves self-taught, have encouraged and supported teachers in these schools to look beyond language to the curriculum in general. Nevertheless, this section must still begin with a brief statement of reasons for including teaching about Islam or Judaism, as well as Christianity, in schools with Muslim or Jewish pupils.

First, there is the need of the child from the minority group to feel accepted. In human terms he is, but culturally it is possible for him to draw the conclusion, as English working-class children have done, that the ways and values of his parents are to be despised. After all, in school the language, clothes (e.g., turban), dietary customs and beliefs they have given him are ignored if not regarded (e.g., Jewish holidays) as a nuisance! No wonder many Muslim or Sikh teenagers experience severe crises of identity. Teaching about their cultures can contribute to their development of self-esteem, and reassure them that their heritage is not to be despised—and their parents that the aim of British education is not to eradicate all traces of alien ways in an attempt to produce one cultureless, secular society! Secondly, any teacher who takes the trouble to listen to his 'white' pupils (not only teenaged) will soon discover what distorted, prejudiced and dangerously incorrect ideas they have about Jews and other minorities. If ignorance is his enemy, the teacher is likely to feel that he must attempt to provide his pupils with accurate information, at least. Recently, attention has been drawn to a third reason. Sadly, but not surprisingly, Muslim and Sikh children are still being given false information about one another's faith in the mosques and gurdwaras and their own homes. Prejudices worse, if possible, than English Protestant has ever had for Roman Catholic or Jew are still being fostered, and the communalism of the sub-continent is being nurtured in children born in Britain! Teachers, once they are aware of this, might feel a responsibility for attempting to replace malicious gossip with knowledge.

One of the two major difficulties peculiar to teaching in the multi-faith school immediately emerges—the potential divisiveness of what the teacher is doing. All education as opposed to indoctrination is subject to this danger. A child from a sheltered home will hear swearing and learn dirty jokes, whilst another will be encouraged to value literacy and enjoy poetry, music and art. The son of a Humanist will encounter Christianity. That Aurangzeb is to Muslims an example of pious orthodoxy and to Sikhs a tyrant needs to be recognised, and also that Gandhi and Jesus in their different ways are controversial figures. 'Jesus Christ' is a term not acceptable to a Jew, though it is to a Muslim.

The knowledge of the child from a minority faith is the other difficulty. The teacher may be fearful of making a mistake and being corrected by a Sikh or Hindu child. The chances are greatest from Jews or Muslims, though being brought up to respect their teachers they may well remain silent. Argument is more likely to come from a Humanist home primed to counter those statements of belief which some Christian teachers still put forward as matters of indisputable fact. Of the solutions offered to teachers apprehensive of a pupil's greater knowledge the most commendable seems to be that of adopting the role of a partner in learning. In no situation should the teacher set himself up as the authoritative fount of knowledge, especially in this one. If he can work with the group of Muslim or Hindu children and help them to tell the class about their prayers, festivals or beliefs, he will have overcome the danger of being shown up and at the same time have adopted a sound teaching method. In support it is hoped that the books and audio-visual aids used will be generally acceptable to the minority group and that their help will be obtained in providing a speaker, arranging a visit to the place of worship or organising an exhibition.

In terms of methodology it would seem that the main difference between teaching Judaism, for example, in a class which has some Jewish members and one in which only Christianity is represented lies in the use one makes of the potential Jewish contribution. The materials should be very much the same, the best available—best, that is, in terms of presenting the faith as a Jew would have it stated. Whether a Jew is present or not, it should be done as if one were. One should never talk about a faith in a manner that one would not adopt were an adherent of it present—nothing should be said about Judaism behind a Jew's back which would not be said to his face. This essential criterion applies to Jehovah's Witnesses and Mormons too.

Both method and content would differ in another way in the multi-faith school. In a so-called Christian school several factors might influence choice of content, and the method might be to study one faith after another. In a school of Muslims, Jews and Humanists as well as Christians the choice of minimum content is to some extent determined. The approach can scarcely be that of Christianity first and then, for two terms at 14 +, Judaism followed by Islam with a visit from a Humanist a year later when the pupils are old enough! Almost immediately the teacher is obliged to make some response to the composition of the class.

'Why doesn't Yaqub eat pork sausages?'
'Why does Jameda wear "trousers"?'
'Why does Sidney Levy say they don't have Christmas in his house, Miss?'
'What is a Jew, Miss?'

These are questions which are posed by first-school children in a multi-faith school. As they grow older, more suspiciously a Muslim boy is likely to ask, 'Why do we only learn about Christianity?' and he will conclude that the reason is because the teacher wishes to convert him. Some Christians still see the aim of RE as being that of putting the Gospel in front of children clearly and simply so that they may have a chance to accept it or reject it. Understandably, such teachers are bemused at the inclusion of other faiths in the syllabus. Those pupils who come from countries which have been areas of strong missionary activity are equally bewildered at being told that the purpose of learning about religion in schools is not evangelism or conversion but understanding. Dialogue is a comparatively recent activity, still the preserve of a sophist minority. A disinterested approach to the study of religion has, in the same way, been a rare activity. We should not expect Muslims new to Britain to appreciate this open-endedness without some suspicion, any more than we should expect it of indigenous Humanists and Jews—especially when the one corporate activity of the school still is, or should be by law, an act of Christian worship!

To return to the questions posed above. What replies can be given?

Each has its simple answer: 'Yaqub or Jameda are Muslims'; 'Sidney is a Jew'; 'A Jew is. . . .' Perhaps that one isn't so easy, but sometimes with young children a simplistic formula is employed such as 'Jews are people who don't believe in Jesus' (which must include the majority of Britons nowadays). All these responses pre-suppose considerable existing knowledge of what a Muslim or a Jew is, yet in the young child only folk-knowledge exists, frequently anti-Paki or anti-Semitic. This the child, by implication, is invited to attach to Jameda, Yaqub or Sidney. Far better with younger pupils would seem to be answers couched in positive, affective terms rather than cognitive and theological. A topic 'Things People Eat' could cover similarities and differences, acquaint children with cultural peculiarities, our dependence on farmers in other lands, and perhaps introduce them to new foods such as chapattis, burfi, or Hamantaschen. They might learn that some societies eat fish as their only meat; that others will not eat meat at all; some will eat the flesh of some animals; all apparently have some restrictions—dogs and snails don't seem to go down very well with most Britons!

'The Clothes People Wear' is a topic which fascinates most first-school pupils, especially if they can make clothes for their own dolls or manufacture and dress pipe-cleaner figures for an Indian village or a costume parade. Drapers' shops will often give teachers oddments and leftovers, and some of those obtained from Asian stores have silver and gold threads, wonderful colours and sometimes a bit of mirror-work. Children may have costume dolls at home which they can bring to create further stimulus. Similarly 'Our Homes' might look at festivals, family life, names and customs, but again in very down-to-earth terms, assembling Eid, Diwali, Jewish New Year and Christmas cards and concentrating on what happens rather than why. Through such topics one hopes that differences will come to be accepted positively as interesting and important, providing variety long before their particular significance can be understood.

Nothing has yet been said of religious stories. They are, of course, the stuff of every faith and the means by which moral and doctrinal tenets are transmitted. However, the teacher needs to ask a number of questions before using them.

Is her aim the transmission of religious beliefs or moral ideas or cultural folk-lore? If it is the first, are these really being conveyed and can they be understood by the pupils? Telling the story of Noah must include the Covenant, the Nativity of Jesus must include the virginal conception, if theological requirements are to be met—if they are to be religious stories, that is. Emasculated of their theology they become cultural folk-lore, important in the child's education but not part of religious education. In a multi-faith or pluralist society one might mention the wisdom of providing hostages to fortune. If some of the indigenous population find stories about the infant Nanak or Krishna far-fetched, may not Muslims find Judaeo-Christian narratives equally peculiar? Furthermore, those children who come from homes where there is no religious belief of any kind and no respect for religion might regard them as amusing or ridiculous. Religious stories, places and objects, as well as sacred songs, pandits, rabbis or vicars, owe their respected status to the beliefs of either individuals or society at large. Britain is no longer such a society.

The use of stories to transmit moral ideas might be more acceptable, to show that moral courage, forgiveness, caring are virtues world-wide, but two comments must be made. First, it is not through knowledge that people become moral. Jesus said, 'Love your enemies,' but Christians have been known to be vindictive. The cliché is true; morality is caught not taught. Neither mottoes nor sermonising produce schools in which human virtues are to be found. Secondly, children have been known to say, 'O.K. God said, "Thou shalt not steal"; but I don't believe in God, so I can pinch things if I like!'

Religious stories in the first school should, it seems, play a supporting role in RE, be used sparingly, and each one should be used only after considerable thought. Their use now needs to be justified where once it was taken for granted.

In the middle years 'Where We Worship' might provide a first introduction to religious practices other than the domestic and social celebrations which accompany festivals, births and weddings. Visits to places of worship often stimulate 9-, 10- or 11-year-olds not only to make models or draw pictures, but also to talk and write about their experiences. The visit to any empty synagogue or gurdwara proves interesting because it is different; the value is enhanced if good guides are available (i.e., those who can talk to children), and of course film-strips or slides accompanied by such sounds as the Muslim call to prayer or the singing of bhajans in a Hindu temple go far towards providing the authenticity which can only be obtained fully by attending an act of worship. One must remember that for many Hindus or Sikhs a visit to a Christian church is also novel and interesting, and that for the child from a traditional English home it is perhaps no less strange.

From the places of worship, besides moving towards ways of worshipping, it is also natural to progress towards books used in worship (hymn-books as well as sacred texts) and to the people through whom the particular faith was revealed. The last of the middle-school years, in many ways, provides an appropriate time for gathering together the fragmentary knowledge of various kinds, geographical and historical as well as religious, which has been acquired since the age of five.

The upper years, from 13 to 16, are those when the teacher might try to probe as far as possible in assisting the student to understand what it means in terms of practices, belief or commitment to be a Jew, a Muslim or a Christian. This might be done, as the Birmingham Syllabus (1975) suggests, through courses on individual religions chosen in such a way that the pupil would study the dominant religion of the culture, Christianity, another religion (probably his own if his background were not Christian) and perhaps an interpretation of life which was not religious. Two snags are obvious. The first is the staffing of courses once any element of choice is introduced in a department with only one or two members of staff. The second is the objection of parents to their children being allowed to choose a course on Humanism or Marxism, options which many Asians and Christians, especially from Eastern Europe (and these form considerable minorities in our larger cities), view with astonishment and dismay.

A preferable approach might be a continuation of the thematic one. Where and when people worship and how they worship is incomplete without answering the questions why do Muslims, Christian denominations or Sikhs worship in their various ways and why do people worship at all, recognising that forms of worship vary and that Humanists and others do not engage in this activity. Here the emphasis is shifting from the practices in themselves to the beliefs which lie behind them, an essential progression if depth is to be achieved and justice done to the various faiths and to the pupils' education. Too often traditional Christian RE has spent its time and energy arguing the historicity of the Resurrection, whilst neglecting to explain any of the meanings which Christians attach to it. This defect must not be repeated and multiplied in the multi-faith school.

Dialogue

The high school should not necessarily be regarded as an opportunity for dialogue, but even if this is not the intention it might well become a reality. After all, it has often happened in the past between the student who would not accept the moral or religious position being stated and the teacher-apologist. Often this was rather like bear-baiting. If the teacher can now act as an organiser and resource guide, helping the Muslim or Humanist students to obtain and assemble their material, there is no reason why such topics as prayer, life after death, or the concept of God should not be explored and serious questions asked about the purpose of religion and the meaning of life itself. There can be little that is more fascinating than hearing a group of Jewish pupils explaining why they cannot accept the messiahship of Jesus, or a Christian student explaining to a Muslim what Jesus means to him. Of course, such a topic as suffering may be beyond the abilities of most teenagers, even sixth-formers, and so might mysticism. They may lack both the knowledge and the personal awareness of the issues. Nevertheless, there are many points at which the uncertainties and perplexities of existence impinge upon the teenager, and one does not have to be a theologian to be concerned about them or highly intelligent to discuss them. Through concern and the need to convey ideas to others as well as the interest which can be aroused through encountering unfamiliar practices and beliefs, theological education and coherent articulation of ideas can be developed.

The multi-faith school, at every age, is potentially a place for growth and enrichment of a kind never before experienced in Britain. Through it the study of world religions can become more than an armchair intellectual exercise. All high schools in Britain are multi-faith in the sense of being pluralist in belief and values. Though this is not the same as having a variety of religions, it presents similar potential for dialogue, the same need to present Christianity coherently and fully in its many dimensions. It makes the same demands upon the teacher to help the pupils understand and articulate their beliefs or disbeliefs. It requires from all, teachers and students alike, a respectful spirit of inquiry in place of the childish curiosity of earlier years. For various reasons some of them, both teachers and pupils, may not wish to share in exchanges which they feel might put their faith at risk or subject it to questioning. Dialogue cannot be forced and, rather than subject a whole class to it, there is a case for organising a lunch-time or after-school discussion group.

Chapter 9

Dialogue and Religious Education

'I think it's silly—men wearing turbans,' said one boy after visiting a Sikh gurdwara. On another occasion a boy said, 'It's daft—Jews not eating pork. We can eat anything we like, can't we, Sir!' These two comments show that the teacher of world religions in school is engaged in some form of dialogue, whether he likes it or not. Indeed, something which is dialogue, though the name may be too posh to describe the rough reality, lies at the very heart of the education of children. RE, whenever it has been anything but catechetical or the reading of the Bible round the class, has always had some element of 'Do you really believe that Jesus rose from the dead, Sir?' or 'Why could God let his son die like that?' and often it has become more personal, especially in the area of human suffering.

World religions have introduced an added dimension—Sikhs or Jews and their beliefs and practices. The purpose of studying Sikhism or Judaism is not to provide dialogue, but in school it is an almost inescapable consequence, even when there are no Sikhs or Jews in the class—as in the schools where the comments quoted above were made. The second of these raises something additional to the first, and perhaps it had better be dealt with first. 'We can eat anything we like, can't we, Sir!'—it was more a defiant statement than a question. I would not have described the boy as a Christian. He didn't go to church, he spent much of his time in RE lessons allied to the hosts of Midian and usually leading them. But on this occasion he used the word 'we'. Over our bacon and eggs he and I were one. Even in a mono-ethnic school world religions, like a study of the Second World War or French civilisation, can introduce an 'us'-and-'them' element which may reveal prejudices or may, as in this example, cause pupils who belong to no side to take sides. (Incidentally, the pork-eating episode raised an interesting precept and practice point which is often overlooked when teaching world religions. We assume that Muslims or Hindus behave and believe as the book says they do because, very often, we only know Islam and Hinduism from books. Christians living by their Book are not free to eat anything they like—but how many really do take Acts, 15:20, seriously!) However, to return to the main point of both stories, the teacher is often thrown into a dialogue situation willy-nilly. How should he respond?

To agree or disagree is easy and so obviously bad that the teacher is likely to do something else. Perhaps hide behind his non-commitment to Sikhism or Judaism: 'Well, of course, I'm not a Sikh, so I must admit the turban seems a little odd to me, but I wouldn't go so far as to use the word "silly".' Of course not, he's a nice liberal chap, the RE teacher. I'd prefer him to say, 'Let's find out why Sikh men wear turbans or Jews don't eat pork,' to engage in education rather than opinion-swapping. Better still, we need to have as a basic aim the search for understanding, so that the pupil realises that we are trading in knowledge and empathy rather than making uninformed, or even informed, value judgements. Prayer might provide a different example, and one which indicates my aim and also the difficulties which can lie in the way of achieving it. The Muslim prayer positions could be presented as odd, almost gymnastic, postures. The pupil needs to understand that they are part of a received tradition to be revered, that Muhammad and his Companions prayed in the same way, and that the acts are accompanied by thoughts, beliefs and especially attitudes which should be in the mind of the person praying. Appreciating these is more important than knowing the postures—both to the pupils and in the teaching of Islam. With 14- and 15-year-olds, the ones most likely to snigger, the study needs to move from positions to the meaning of prayer in Islam. With younger children, at least, the importance of prayer in Islam can be stressed by references to preparation, orientation and the many ways in which it is not to be undertaken lightly in normal circumstances. Now for a difficulty. Jesus never taught his followers prayer positions. He simply said don't be ostentatious and gave them a prayer. This need not mean that he regarded posture as unimportant; his followers were all Jews, they already had a tradition, unlike the first Muslims. However, as time passed, Christians adopted a variety of prayer positions, especially from the time of the Reformation. Postures appeared more important than mental and spiritual attitudes. The inheritors of those traditions and quarrels are in our schools; the willingness to denounce rituals as 'silly' or worse is deep-rooted. Moreover, when the teacher reaches Christian prayer the lapsed Catholic is likely to defend kneeling against the lapsed Methodist who says it is not necessary. In a religion which has seen members of a denomination split into two congregations over the installation of a musical instrument to accompany hymn-singing one must be aware of the difficulties which stand in the way of an empathetic study of religion. Nevertheless, it is a necessary task which the teacher must not avoid as part of his own education and then that of his pupils!

Once we have ceased religious soliloquising we have opened the gates to dialogue. We may still soliloquise at 'O' or 'A' level or in higher-education courses where we simply transfer knowledge from one person to others, but if our teaching is effective by being thought-provoking if not attitude-changing soliloquy is not possible. Once we have introduced world religions, or even if we stick to Bible-teaching in our pluralistic, secular Britain, soliloquies or monologues are not possible. It is not necessary to have Muslims or Jews in the class for dialogue to take place. Nowadays hostility to any orthodoxy is so acceptable that teenaged education students from working-class backgrounds who are radicals in college can be seen valiantly defending what are regarded as 'middle-class' values like racial equality or prison reform against youngsters only five years their junior from identical backgrounds! However, in the multi-faith school dialogue is of a different sort. Instead of the teacher attempting to widen and deepen knowledge, he is a catalyst encouraging peer learning. There are pupils who know what it is like to be a Muslim or a Jew sitting in front of him. His task is to help them share their beliefs and experiences and explain their practices. They may lack knowledge and articulation; his role is to help them to obtain resource material and use it. There is now no lack of reliable audio-visual aids and text-books produced by Jews, Muslims and Sikhs or people collaborating with them. Hinduism lags some way behind, and Buddhism is a virtual non-starter. Because peer learning is so important, because the Jewish or Christian child is potentially the greatest aid to the teacher, it is desperately important that parents should not withdraw their children from RE but should encourage them to play a full part in the lessons. It is equally important, of course, that the multi-faith school should make their participation possible and encourage it, something which is unlikely to happen unless pupils learn about the faiths which are represented in the school.

The teacher has normally been regarded as the fountain of know-ledge, if not of wisdom. If peer learning is to take place, or if pupils are to satisfy their own searches for meaning, he must change his stance. He must be a catalyst aiding those who are in search of know-ledge or meaning in their quests and provoking them and others to realise that there is a search to be made and that there are problems and solutions. Instead of standing at the front of the class with his Bible, Qur'an or Christian Education Movement Probe *Woman and Man* in his hand, giving answers or defending the faith, he is standing alongside them and among them, still sometimes directing but more often sharing and not acting as an authority or a mediator. If he can work in this way and help his pupils to understand that he has not become a faceless, opinionless purveyor of work-cards but that education is more than exchanging opinions and rejecting the authori-tative statement of teachers, he is also likely to feel happier teaching about Judaism with Jewish boys in the class than he was when he stood at the front of the class and anxiously handed out information which he hoped was correct!

Dialogue is also likely to take place when pupils at fifth- or sixth-form level examine concepts of God or beliefs about death and whether anything lies beyond it. Here they are embarking upon the only form of comparative religion which is now regarded as acceptable. Its purpose is not to evaluate but to discover how different faiths approach a common issue—for example, human death. In the process the student will discover what Humanists believe as well as the teachings of Christianity and Hinduism.

At the beginning of this section it was suggested that in school, where our concern is for children as much as (I would say more than) pure knowledge, dialogue between the child and experience, the child and knowledge, the teacher and the child, the child and his peers, is a constant activity which the teacher is promoting, observing, sometimes structuring. Because religious education in Britain has been a concern of the Christian churches and still is through the machinery of the 1944 Act, there has been, outside the schools but influencing them, inter-denominational dialogue leading to the production of Agreed Syllabuses of Religious Instruction. In recent years the Roman Catholics have begun to share in what was formerly a Free Church-Anglican exercise, but generally, and I hope permanently, the denominations have left RE in maintained schools to the specialists. A new dialogue has taken its place. The Religious Education Council and the Standing Conference on Inter-Faith Dialogue in Religious Education are indicative of the feeling that in the multi-faith United Kingdom of the late twentieth century issues are inter-faith rather than inter-denominational. Those exchanges of views which have so far taken place in meetings and courses convened by these bodies suggest that educational rather than faith considerations could continue to dominate the curriculum development of religious education as they have done to an increasing extent since the mid-1960s, but for many years these bodies will have a valuable part to play in providing opportunities for people of different faiths to meet and exchange views, to grow in trust and mutual understanding and to act as a reminder that, whatever its name, and however separate from the mission field, the mosque or gurdwara it may be, it has still to do with the beliefs of living people.

POSTSCRIPT

Eric Sharpe* has distinguished four types of dialogue. It might help teachers to be aware of these divisions. Dr Sharpe's view is that essential to all dialogue is commitment, a standpoint.

(1) Discursive Dialogue. This is intellectual inquiry based on sympathy and respect for one another's views, accurate knowledge of one's own beliefs and scrupulous honesty in presenting one's own views and listening to those of others.

(2) Human Dialogue, the meeting of people on a purely human level, a sympathetic encounter in a friendly atmosphere. This need not be religious; people are doing it all the time.

(3) Secular Dialogue. Here the emphasis is on the common problems which face mankind—population, hunger, war, leprosy, injustice—rather than upon the issues which divide it.

(4) Interior Dialogue. This might be called a meeting of souls and probably depends on a belief that ultimately Reality is one and all faiths emanate the one and lead to the one.

Evaluating this chapter in terms of Dr Sharpe's categories, I would say that the basis of the education of children is human dialogue, commitment to the value of human life and to the search for knowledge and meaning. In RE it is specifically to the importance of understanding the place and function of religions (and other belief systems) in human experience.

This can develop into discursive dialogue by accident or design and may, when examining the ethical and social dimensions of belief systems, touch on secular dialogue.

Again, by accident, interior dialogue may be taking place. This is my own experience as I meet with other faiths in my study or teach about them in the classroom, especially when I meet with their adherents or attend a service in a synagogue or gurdwara. However, it is not my *intention* to invite students to engage in such dialogue within themselves or to submit them to it. This type of dialogue, like worship, should be a voluntary activity as far as possible; indeed, it must be, for though I can make someone say the Lord's Prayer I cannot make him pray.

The Goals of Inter-Religious Dialogue in *Truth and Dialogue* ed. John Hick (Sheldon Press, 1974).

Chapter 10

Teaching about Buddhism

The teaching of Buddhism is not unique in having problems, but some of the problems in teaching Buddhism are unique: no God, no soul, no immortal heaven (or hell), etc. It is the purpose of this article, therefore, to point out to prospective teachers of the subject suggested arguments or suggested solutions that can be used when these problems arise. Personally, I often find analogy to be one of the best ways to 'explain' a Buddhist concept which is otherwise inconceivable to my pupils. On the basis of some modest success, I would humbly advise fellow-teachers to use the same method. The further purpose of the article is to help you set parameters about which areas should be taught, and which others can be left *if* you are teaching below 'A' level. It will be noted that throughout I have used Buddhist Pali terms, usually in brackets. I give these for your information, and would suggest that an excessive use of them in lessons, certainly below 'A' level, would be counter-productive. Some, however, such as *anatta, Nibbana, kamma* and *bhikkhu* (which I would suggest is preferable to 'monks'), are either necessary because virtually untranslatable, or would be useful to give the pupils something of the 'feel' of the religion.

In a letter to the *Times Educational Supplement* in 1974 one correspondent stated the belief that religion begins with God. There have been several definitions of 'religion' in the history of the study of religions, and most of them would seem to take this or a similar stance. If, then, to be a religion a system of beliefs has to include the idea of a supreme being responsible for the creation of the universe, and capable of manifesting itself, by one means or another, in history, this effectively excludes Buddhism; and yet in books on world *religions* Buddhism is always included, even though it has neither need nor concern for God. If God exists, then he too is within the realms of rebirth (*samsara*), and will at some future time be reborn so that he too may reach a stage where his own cycle of rebirths will cease. However, in this age of analysis and categorisation one is almost compelled to place Buddhism somewhere; but where? If it *must* be labelled, then let that label read 'non-theistic religion'.*

Since God does not hold an important place in Buddhism, who or

---

*This is part of the title of a book published several years ago: *Buddhism—A Non-Theistic Religion*. See bibliography.

what do Buddhists worship? There are numerous pictures of adherents of this faith in what most people would describe as acts of worship before statues of the Buddha. Not to split hairs, 'veneration' would be a better word, since prayers and requests to him would be useless. Because he has attained *Nibbana*,* he is beyond communication in either direction; and for those who insist that *something*, no matter how vague, can be said about Buddha's after-life condition, the following can be given as a conclusive argument:

It is wrong to say he exists.
It is wrong to say he does not exist.
It is wrong to say he both exists and does not exist.
It is wrong to say he neither exists nor does not exist.

Here we have a religion where worship is not needed, where God plays no important role. We seem, therefore, to have found an Eastern Humanism. But, whereas in theory this point may have some validity, in practice what virtually amounts to worship occurs, and the gods do play a role in the daily round of the common man's existence. And in Mahayana Buddhism the help of a whole host of beings is sought in the need to escape from this realm of rebirths. These beings, called *bodhisattvas*,** form part of the distinction between Theravada Buddhism and Mahayana Buddhism. The latter has been compared with a cat carrying her kitten from one place to another, and the former has been compared with a monkey carrying her young. In the example of cats, the kitten is quite passive; but the young monkey must play some active role since, while his mother does most of the work, he must at least hang on. The interpretation of both these comparisons is that Mahayana Buddhism believes that the individual will gain salvation mainly through the intermediary of the *bodhisattvas*; whereas Theravada Buddhism believes more in a policy of self-help—the individual is entirely responsible for his own condition, and will therefore bring about his own release, using the Buddha's teachings, from further rebirths.

The differences between Theravada and Mahayana Buddhism provide a considerable problem in the teaching of Buddhism. For an

---

*It is impossible to know what verb to place before *Nibbana*. Does one gain, attain, realise or enter it? Since *Nibbana* is totally beyond any meaningful definition, the answer cannot be known, and any verb used, therefore, is merely a literary expedient. The Pali texts do not help: the word describing the Buddha's death is *parinibbayi* (*Dighanikaya*, Book II: 156) which only takes us straight back to the problem.

**Literally, 'enlightenment beings'. They are capable of attaining *Nibbana*, but they have vowed not to do so until all mankind has been 'saved'.

'A' level course these would need to be dealt with, though not in depth. Any teaching before 'A' level might need to note some of the differences, but a detailed knowledge of them would be unnecessarily time-consuming with probably a minimum return. What, then, can be taught? The corollary to this question is: What do the Theravada and Mahayana schools hold in common? Since we are searching for a simple answer to the question, that answer would be: A traditional life of the Buddha, the Four Noble Truths, the Noble Eightfold Path, the *Paticcasamuppada*, rebirth, *kamma, anatta* and *Nibbana*.*

That the Buddha existed need not be doubted; but *when* he lived— that is a problem. Several dates have been suggested, supported by arguments that need not concern us. However, those often quoted by Western scholars are 563-483 B.C.E.; and, since the matter is largely academic, it may be left.** In any case, the age of the Buddha at the time of his death is consistently given as 80 years.

The traditional versions of his life are replete with supernatural happenings; and the life-style of his early years was one of luxury, splendour and riches. By tradition his father was a powerful king ruling a Himalayan kingdom around the southern border of present-day Nepal. The reality, however, may have been less splendid since the word *raja* could equally mean a tribal chieftain. The details of his life need not be laid out here since they are easily available elsewhere; but in reading any of the versions, either from the original or secondary sources, the reader may wish to keep in mind the fact that these details do vary, sometimes to the point of contradiction. For example, one version states that he was delivered into the world while his mother was standing up; another version has him coming from his mother's side.***

For the next twenty-nine years Siddhattha Gotama lived a life of extreme luxury; but, more than this, his father kept him from all the sorrows of the world such as sickness, old age and death. He only knew of their existence when, in his twenty-ninth year, he saw examples of each of these three ills by accident (or by design of the

---

*It goes without saying that a detailed study of this question of commonality would bring out far more information, but not every teacher who wants to teach world religions has the need (or the time) for an in-depth knowledge of Buddhism.

**Other dates include 623-543 B.C.E., 624-544 B.C.E. (Theravada); 566-486 B.C.E., 558-478 B.C.E. (Mahayana).

***Neither of these is impossible. Western culture, being used to its own version of obstetrics, does not often realise that not all women have their babies in a prone position. The second alternative is possible if it is thought of in terms of a caesarean section, an operation being carried out in the eighth century B.C.E., though the women, it seems, rarely survived the operation until the sixteenth century C.E. This last point supports, if only in a small way, the possibility of a caesarean section, since his mother died seven days after his birth.

gods, depending upon which version of the traditional life-story one is reading). On each of these occasions Gotama was stunned when his charioteer told him that he too was subject to these things. A fourth occasion, however, brought a happier encounter when he saw a holy man, a wanderer who had given up home and possessions in his search for release from rebirth. Now Gotama realised two things: there was suffering in the world, and there was a means available to escape this suffering. Soon after learning these two facts he too left his home and family. He doffed his rich and refined clothes to don the meagre garb of a beggar; and so began six years of intensive search.*

During this period he visited two teachers of some merit, Uddaka Ramaputta and Alara Kalama; but neither of them supplied satisfactory answers, even though Gotama was able to master their teachings within a very short time. Leaving them, he joined up with five other ascetics, who eventually looked to him as their leader. However, they left him some time later when they thought him to be returning to the *dolce vita* once more, this decision being rather hastily made when they saw him accepting a bowl of food from a young woman after a long period of virtual starvation. But this was not, as they thought, a giving up of the quest: Gotama had merely decided that the following of either extreme—too much or too little—was not conducive to obtaining his goal. From now on he was to walk the middle path between these two.

Soon after this, following several years of weary toil, he sat down under a tree—later to be known as the Bodhi Tree, in a place later to be known as Bodh Gaya—and vowed that he would not move from that place until he had discovered the elusive answer. It was then that Mara** came to Gotama in order to try to tempt him from his resolve. All manner of means were used: words, weapons, threats, and, finally, his three daugthers, Passion, Desire and Discontent; but each and every one failed, and Mara retreated in defeat. On that night Siddhattha Gotama achieved success, and with that success a title: Buddha, a word meaning 'one who has gained knowledge'. What that knowledge was we shall look at in a moment.

Once he had studied his new-found knowledge, he sought out the five ascetics who had recently left him. At first they were reluctant to receive him but, in spite of themselves, they listened, and consequently became his first followers. After this the new teaching spread very quickly, until all manner of people were involved, from beggars to

*In the *Ariyapariyesana sutta* of the *Majjhima Nikaya* there is another version of the Buddha's going forth from the home to the homeless state, and this strongly suggests that he was rather younger than 29 when he left home.
**Sometimes referred to as the Buddhist Devil.

kings. Some became *bhikkhus* (monks), while others remained as lay-followers.

A definitive chronological biography is impossible, though educated guesses could be made.* Inevitably, examples of miracles can be found, both during his boyhood and adult life. These may be added to lessons to make the narrative of his life less boring; but whether they are to be regarded as distorted history of real events, or additions made by later biographers—thus making the interesting distinction between history *wie es eigentlich gewesen* ('history as it really was') and history *wie es eigentlich geworden* ('history as it actually became'; i.e., through the interpretation or bias of the historian)—is a matter which need only concern those who are involved in an in-depth study—usually at university level—of this subject. Most of his forty-five-year ministry, however, was spent in preaching, teaching and advising. He was freely available to anyone who wanted to see him, even up to the moment of his death, when a wanderer, Subhadda, took this last chance to hear the Buddha's answer to his question.

Before dying, the Buddha gave explicit instructions to his *bhikkhus* concerning the manner of how his body was to be dealt with. He also gave them a short sermon which can be briefly summed up in the sentiment 'From now on you're on your own. Only diligent effort will bring success in achieving release from rebirths.'

Let us now look briefly at some of the basic teachings of this man— and that was what he was, a *man* and not a god. There are several versions of his enlightenment, and each of these versions gives a different account of what it was that constituted his new-found knowledge. But this is a problem merely to be stated and not studied in an article of this nature. For argument's sake, let us assume—and it must be emphasised that, when all the pros and cons have been stated, it is an assumption—that the Buddha formulated the Four Noble Truths and the Noble Eightfold Path. In any teaching of Buddhism these must be explained first of all since they are the foundations for all the other teachings.

The Truths have on occasion been justifiably compared with the principles of medical diagnosis: identification of the disease, its cause, its cure, and the means for bringing about the cure. The *first truth* states that all life is suffering.** It has to be stressed that this is not a

*See, for example, G. P. Malalasekere, *Dictionary of Pali Proper Names* (London 1960), 'Gotama'.

**'Suffering' is often used as a 'translation' of the Pali word *dukkha*, but the latter is virtually beyond translation. Any English word used, therefore, be it 'suffering', 'anguish', 'dis-ease', etc., gives only a hint of what is meant. None can be used as a 'be-all-end-all' term.

pessimistic outlook. To refer back to the medical analogy, a doctor is not a prophet of doom if he tells the patient that he is ill. This would only be the case if he failed to suggest a cure. Such is the situation in Buddhism: the Buddha pointed out that all life is suffering—physical and mental suffering—no matter what the condition of the individual, because, and this is the *second noble truth*, everyone desires something or other and, even if our desires are fulfilled, we are still not ultimately happy since there is a part of us which either craves more or is concerned about the eventual passing away of our present happy state. In the final analysis, *nothing* is permanent, all things are subject to decay. But to some this basic point that we are all subject to suffering is seen to be contradicted by the fact that there are people in the world who suffer remarkably little. In giving a counter-argument to this observation we have to realise that we are not confining ourselves to the Semitic idea of just one life for each person. Buddhism, remember, includes the concept of rebirth; and it has been stated in this regard that the amount of tears each person has shed in his rebirths would be enough to make an ocean!

If, then, suffering has its origins in the fact that each person constantly desires this and that, it follows naturally, as stated in the *third noble truth*, that the end of desire is the end of suffering. Even a moment's thought will show just how difficult the cessation of desire can be. The ultimate difficulty, of course, is how does one solve the seeming paradox of desiring to stop desire? But the answer is something that cannot be given to common lay-folk, since it lies in experience and not in a clever assemblage of words. In the beginning of the process, however, the method can be given some explanation in that it involves the Noble Eightfold Path (= the *fourth noble truth*), and words can be used to explain what that means.

To state the obvious, the Path is divided into eight parts. However, there is a secondary division, this time into three parts under the headings Morality (*sila*), Concentration (*samadhi*) and Wisdom (*panna*):

(1)	Right Understanding	III
(2)	Right Thought	WISDOM
(3)	Right Speech	I
(4)	Right Action	MORALITY
(5)	Right Livelihood	
(6)	Right Effort	II
(7)	Right Mindfulness	CONCENTRATION
(8)	Right Concentration	

It can be seen from the table just given that the order changes slightly with the secondary division; and for teaching purposes the latter, I would suggest, is the one to follow. Eventually, the whole Path is to be practised simultaneously, but in the beginning it seems inevitable that some kind of sequential process should be followed,* and therefore the order we shall follow in giving a brief analysis of each of the parts is the secondary one.

Right Speech
There is both a negative and a positive side to this section, as also to several of the others. Negatively, it does not allow telling lies, spreading gossip, slander, or indulging in frivolous chatter. All speech should be motivated with the best of intentions, and with regard to other people's feelings. For instance, if criticism is really needed, it should be given kindly and compassionately, free from any wish to hurt. In short, one should not speak just to hear one's own voice, but for an intended moral purpose; and, if this condition cannot be fulfilled, then one should maintain a 'noble silence'.

Right Action
Three things in particular should be avoided: killing, stealing and sexual misconduct. The first prohibition includes *all* living beings, no matter what the circumstances.** This should mean that all Buddhists should be vegetarians; but in practice this is not always by any means the case—not even with the *bhikkhus* who must eat whatever is put into their begging-bowls, so long as they are not aware that any meat that might be placed there has been killed explicitly for their sake.

Stealing may be left as self-explanatory, though a Buddhistic analysis of the term can make it mean far more than usual.***

Sexual misconduct, when it refers to the lay-man, means no pre-marital and no extra-marital sexual intercourse. For the *bhikkhu*, it means no carnal knowledge of any sort; and, if this precept is disobeyed, it is followed by summary dismissal from the monastery.

Right Livelihood
It follows from what has been said that certain occupations are necessarily barred to Buddhists. In the texts these are stated as being the selling of weapons, humans into slavery, animals for slaughter,

---

*Here I must admit to giving opinion rather than fact.

**See Winston L. King, *In the Hope of Nibbana*, p. 136, on the dilemma arising from a snake about to kill a child.

***See Piyadassi Thera, *The Buddha's Ancient Path*, p. 148. This book is thoroughly recommended as an extremely lucid and easily understandable study of the Four Noble Truths and the Noble Eightfold Path.

intoxicating drinks and poisons. Buddhists are also told to refrain from 'slaughtering, fishing, soldiering, deceit, treachery, soothsaying, trickery, usury, etc.'*

Right Effort
This involves mental rather than physical effort, in that the person is told to rid himself of any evil thoughts that are present and prevent the arising of any other evil thoughts in the future. At the same time good thoughts must be retained, and other good thoughts are to be created.

Right Mindfulness
Perhaps, of all the divisions of the Path, this in its way is one of the hardest. It involves awareness of oneself. More often than not, people can describe the outside world, but when asked to describe themselves with equal objectivity either they become quaintly reticent or their answers give a distorted description. A proper application of right mindfulness means that the person becomes aware of himself by degrees, aware of all the actions he performs, including breathing, walking, sitting down, eating, etc., and all the thoughts and feelings he has. At first this has to be done as a conscious effort, but after a time the process becomes automatic, leading on to the next stage.

Right Concentration
Extending the discipline created under Right Mindfulness, Right Concentration means to concentrate on one thought only, to the exclusion of all other distractions.

The two remaining divisions, under the general heading of Wisdom, we shall take in their reverse order.

Right Thought
Thoughts which are not free from hatred (*dosa*), greed (*lobha*) and delusion (*moha*) can never hope to gain a proper understanding of the Buddha's teachings. He taught that all things are impermanent, and therefore it is vanity of vanities to desire something which cannot bring permanent joy. Temporary happiness brings suffering in its wake. So, putting aside hatred and greed, because nothing in this world is worth such emotions, the adherent should engender thoughts of loving-kindness (*metta*), compassion (*karuna*), altruistic joy (*mudita*) and equanimity (*upekkha*) toward all living beings.

Right Understanding
This is possibly the most important part of the Path. With it one sees

---

*Nyanatiloka, *Buddhist Dictionary*, '*magga*'.

the world *as it really is*, without preconceived notions and prejudices. Thus, nothing is held to be of intrinsic value, and therefore the wish to possess is eradicated, and with it goes suffering. 'To one endowed with Right Understanding it is impossible to have a clouded view of phenomena, for he is immune from all impurities and has attained the unshakeable deliverance of the mind (*akuppa ceto vimutti*).'*

This 'deliverance of the mind' is the ultimate goal of Buddhism called *Nibbana*. However, there is little else that can be said on this subject, and what is said should, strictly speaking, be in the form of negatives since *no words* can even begin to describe *Nibbana*; and this is where a problem might present itself for some teachers. People, no matter of what age or maturity, often cannot see why a particular something in the area of religion cannot be explained, and conclude from the silence or inadequate efforts of the teacher that the something is a mere figment of the imagination, since anything worthwhile can be described to some degree or other. Here the teacher may find refuge in analogy. Ask a member of the class to close his eyes, and then take out a biro (or whatever), hand it to another member of the class and ask him to describe the colour of the biro without actually using the word for that colour. It will almost immediately be recognised that this is impossible: each colour is a 'thing in itself' (*ding an sich*), beyond definition. Other examples could be cited: describe the taste of an apple—an apple-taste—or an orange—an orange-taste. With such examples demonstrated, the inability to describe *Nibbana* should be more acceptable to the sceptical mind.

But the real stumbling-block in teaching about Buddhism is the belief in rebirth. It should be noted and emphasised that the Buddhists do not accept the Hindu doctrine of the permanent, unchanging soul; and it is wrong, therefore, to talk in terms of 'transmigration' or 'reincarnation' since both assume the existence of a soul. Buddhism divides the individual into five parts ('aggregates'), none of which is permanent, but all are in a constant state of flux. The five are as follows:

1 the body (*rupa*)
2 feelings (*vedana*)
3 perception (*sanna*)
4 kamma formations (*sankhara*)**
5 consciousness (*vinnana*).

*Piyadassi Thera, *The Buddha's Ancient Path*, p. 84.
**This word is virtually impossible to translate. In an article, 'The Translation and Interpretation of the Twelve Terms in the Paticcasamuppada', *NUMEN* (1974), vol. XXI, pp. 40-4, I eventually 'translated' it as 'volitional sustenance', a rather bulky term, and one which I might refine in another context.

The first of these can be taken as self-explanatory: it refers to all the physical parts of the person. The four remaining refer to the mental or ideational part. The order in which they appear in the list is always the same; and the reason for this order is given by the fifth-century C.E. Buddhist scholar, Buddhaghosa:

> *Rupa* is mentioned first because it is easily comprehensible to an average man. As this *rupa* (matter, object) gives rise to a feeling good, bad, or indifferent, so *vedana* is treated as a second *khandha*. As this *vedana* (feeling) directs one's attention to the form and nature of the source of the feeling and thereby engenders *sanna* (perception), so *sanna* is placed next. After *sanna*, happens the accumulation of mental states, hence *sankhara* is treated as the fourth. Though *vinnana* precedes *sankhara* it is mentioned last as it is the most important of the four mental *khandhas* forming, as it does, the basis of *vedana*.*

I am willing to risk the sin of *hubris* by suggesting a different order for the mental aggregates. For the sake of example, let us assume any material object: first of all a person becomes aware of it (*vinnana*), which is followed by perception (*sanna*), i.e., recognition based on previous experiences. Then follows a pleasant, unpleasant or indifferent sensation (*vedana*), the first two of which (at least) stimulate the wish to perform some action (*sankhara*), thus sustaining that person's cycle of existence (*samsara*).

It must be emphasised that all these aggregates are in a constant state of flux, never the same from one moment to the next. The fact that there seems to be some form of permanency is due entirely to delusion. It is scientifically provable that our bodies are changing their state of existence each second with all the chemical reactions that are occurring in them; and our state of mind is always undergoing change. Accepting, then, as one surely must, this process of continuous change, Buddhism extends the argument and says that death is just another part of this process. Indeed, it could be another name for it, since we are 'dying' all the time:

> 'Death' in ordinary usage means 'the disappearance of the vital faculty confined to a single life-time, and therewith of the psycho-physical life-process conventionally called Man, Animal, Personality, Ego' etc. Strictly speaking, however, death is the continually repeated dissolution and vanishing of each momentary

---

*N. Dutt, *Early Monastic Buddhism* (Calcutta, 1971), p. 211. His reference is *Visuddhimagga*, p. 477. *Khandha* is the Pali word often translated as 'aggregates'.

physical-mental combination, and thus it takes place every moment. About this momentaneity [*sic*] of existence, it is said in Vis-(uddhimagga) VIII:

'In the absolute sense, beings have only a very short moment to live, life lasting as long as a single moment of consciousness lasts. Just as a cart-wheel, whether rolling or whether at a standstill, at all times only rests on a single point of its periphery: even so the life of a living being lasts only for the duration of a single moment of consciousness. As soon as that moment ceases the being also ceases. For it is said: "The being of the past moment of consciousness has lived, but it does not exist now, nor will it live in the future. The being of the future moment has not yet lived, nor does it live now, but it will live in the future. The being of the present moment has not lived, it does live just now but it will not live in the future."'*

On this analysis, the need for a soul to transmigrate at death is found to be void. There are examples that can be cited in the hope of making this matter more acceptable. The classic one is to imagine a row of candles. The first one is lit, and then the second from the first, the third from the second, and so on down the line. When the last one is lit from the penultimate candle, the question may then be asked: Is the flame on the last candle the same as, or different from, the flame on the first? The answer is that it both is and is not, since it exists in its own right, but owes its existence to the first flame. A flame is also a good example to illustrate impermanent existence since it is always changing, by its very nature, from one moment to the next, and yet it gives the *impression* of being the same.

Buddhism is always at pains to analyse in order to facilitate understanding, and the process of rebirth does not escape this analysis, as has been seen. But why is there rebirth? The answer is that a person is reborn because of his desires, since these cloud the mind to a proper understanding of the world. Before this is taken further it should be realised that Buddhism—and Hinduism—sees rebirth as a bad thing, and it is the goal of all Buddhists to be released from this cycle. But, in the meantime, most Buddhists—probably all Buddhists, since we never seem to hear of any *arahants* (totally enlightened beings) nowadays—seek a better rebirth, which therefore means that rebirth can also be seen in terms of reward *and* punishment; and this suitably explains the varying fortunes of the human, and animal, population in the world. But how can one go about stopping one's rebirths? Answer: Stop desiring. How does one stop desiring? To this no

*Nyanatiloka, *Buddhist Dictionary*, '*marana*'.

worthwhile answer can be given within the limits of this article, except to say that the means lies within the proper practice of the Noble Eightfold Path, and an understanding of how desire—which can also be called craving—arises. The latter involves an analysis of the *Paticcasamuppada*—a word that has been translated in many ways, but I favour "Dependent Arising". This subject should not be dealt with below 'A' level, since a proper study of it would be time-consuming. More than this, it is complicated and technical, which is a reason why it is not being discussed at any length in this article. Suffice it to say that it is a formula giving the reason for the existence of desire (craving)—due ultimately to ignorance of the true state of the world and man's condition in it—and the consequences of craving, which are future rebirths. The way to stop craving, therefore, is to cease being ignorant (in the Buddhist sense), and the means to stop being ignorant is to follow the Middle Way, one of the titles of the Buddha's teachings.

What follows is a guide to those subjects that can be taught in lessons on Buddhism (see Figure 1). It is by no means exhaustive since it is neither possible, nor needful, to mention all the matters that can be included. The teacher *in situ* is the only one who can decide how much information to give, based on the capabilities of the students. Those subjects that have been mentioned can be dealt with in varying depths, and many of them *necessarily* include topics not mentioned in this article. For example, lessons on the Noble Eightfold Path could—which is not to say should—go much further than a brief résumé of the eight parts. Right Mindfulness, for instance, could include the five Hindrances, the five Aggregates of Clinging, the seven Factors of Enlightenment, and the Four Noble Truths (again). To illustrate the point still further, it is possible in using Nyanatiloka's *Buddhist Dictionary* to start off with virtually any given article and then to find oneself referred backwards and forwards until all the articles have been read, thus showing the very real inter-connection there is between the different teachings and their sub-sections. Use of at least some of the books suggested at the end of the article will show that this problem—if problem it be—is less acute than a reading of this paragraph might suggest.

Order of Subject-matter
(1) *Background information on the social and religious conditions during the Buddha's lifetime.* Being a daughter-religion of Hinduism,* Buddhism cannot be treated in a vacuum since there are both comparisons and contrasts that can be, and sometimes need to be, made between the two.
(2) *Life of the Buddha.* The individual teacher must make up his or

her own mind as to how much place is to be given to the various supernatural happenings that are related in the various traditions. For the higher levels of education it may be worthwhile to note that some of these 'happenings' could have an original basis in history. For example, one birth-story could be related to a caesarean section; and the 'duel' between the Buddha and Mara before the enlightenment could have its origins in the Buddha's own inner temptations and doubts, plus inclement weather.

(3) Apart from the *Paticcasamuppada*, I do not see how any of these could be omitted; and it must be repeated that a lot more could be added.

- (a) The Four Noble Truths
- (b) The Noble Eightfold Path
- (c) The five, eight and ten moral precepts. These have not been mentioned before quite simply because they can offer no problems. (See Piyadassi's book.)
- (d) The life-style of the *bhikkhus*. Not mentioned for the same reason.
- (e) *Kamma (Karma)**
- (f) Rebirth and *Anatta*. The latter is the 'no-soul' or 'no-self' doctrine which has been noted in the article.
- (g) *Nibbana (Nirvana)*

*The first term is in Pali, the language of the Theravada Canon, and the bracketed term is the Sanskrit equivalent which is usually preferred in those books written from a Mahayana bias.

---

*'Hinduism' is a conventional term. Without making this point too complex, it should be noted that the 'Hinduism' of the Buddha's time can more correctly be referred to as Brahmanism; and it was a system of beliefs undergoing developmental change, represented by the teachings in the Upanishads. In this context, examples of some comparisons and contrasts would be:

- (a) *Brahman* and *Nibbana*.
- (b) *Kamma (Karma)*.
- (c) *Atman* and *Anatta*.
- (d) The Hindu belief in reincarnation contrasted with the Buddhist belief in rebirth.
- (e) Later on 'Hinduism' developed the *bhakti* cult, demonstrated by the teaching in the *Bhagavad Gita*, for example. I would suggest that this bears comparison with the *Bodhisatta* beliefs in Mahayana Buddhism.
- (f) Hinduism has no founder, though there were, are, and still can be many personalities who could be picked out as innovators in various areas of belief. Buddhism, of course, did have a founder; and, while it adapts to the contemporary situation, it is my understanding that few, *if any*, innovations have been made for many centuries.
- (g) Both religions—in theory, at least—are extremely tolerant of other belief systems. However, there is still a contrast here in that Hinduism is not a missionary faith, but Buddhism made a deliberate and successful effort to spread itself throughout southern and South-East Asia.

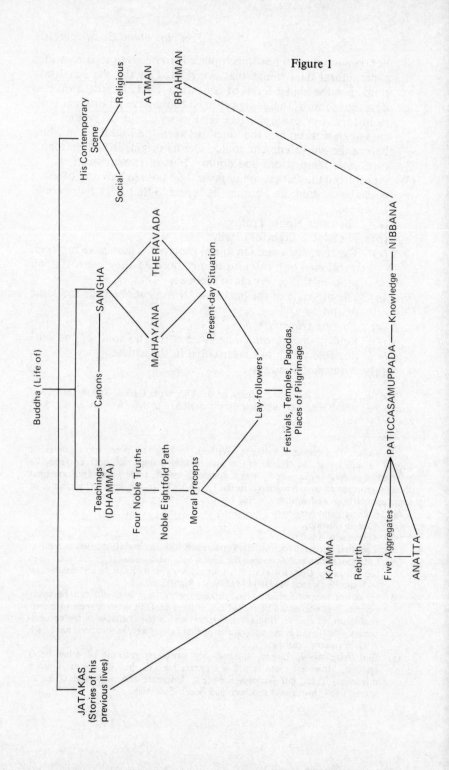

Figure 1

    (*h*)   *Paticcasamuppada (Pratityasamutpada)**
(4) *Development of the Different Schools and the Spread of Buddhism*
    (*a*)   *Hinayana*, which has become present-day *Theravada*: Sri Lanka, Burma, Cambodia, Laos, Thailand.
    (*b*)   *Mahayana*: China, Japan, Mongolia, Vietnam, Korea.
    (*c*)   *Vajrayana*: Tibet.

Inevitably, the Zen tradition will be included. But heed a note of warning. It is possible to describe various things concerning the *practice* of Zen, but little about its teachings. In this context the words 'He who knows does not speak, and he who speaks does not know' should always be borne in mind.

BUDDHISM IN THE MODERN WORLD

This is a difficult subject for at least two reasons. One is the very fluid political situation in South-East Asia at the time of writing. Also, there is very little, from my experience at least, that can be said about Buddhism in Communist China and present-day Tibet. The other, perhaps more practical reason from the classroom teacher's point of view is the dearth of easily available published material on this subject.

Buddhism as it is supposed to be and Buddhism as it actually *is* practised do differ at the grass-roots level, and the average non-intellectual Buddhist can hold certain beliefs and follow certain practices which are not orthodox, to say the least of it. Unfortunately, I have never had the privilege of visiting a Buddhist country, and so I must rely on those rare sources of information that have been published, particularly M. E. Spiro's *Buddhism and Society* (see bibliography).

The philosophy of Buddhism is all too often too complex for the average Buddhist. He has not had the time to be trained in understanding the intricate doctrines of the scriptures, and instead lives in a world based on tradition, a tradition that may go back to a time before Buddhism became a prominent feature in his country. The Buddhism that he practises, therefore, is hybrid, and the goal(s) he

---

*A subject not always dealt with in any great detail, important though it is. The British Mahabodhi Society, London Buddhist Vihara, 5 Heathfield Gardens, London W4 4JU, might be able to supply you, at very reasonable cost, with copies of the following booklets:
Piyadassi Thera, *Dependent Origination* (Kandy, 1959).
Nyanatiloka Mahathera, *The Significance of Dependent Origination in Theravada Buddhism* (Kandy, 1969).
Bhikkhu Khantipala, *The Wheel of Birth and Death* (Kandy, 1970).

wishes to achieve may be some way from the Buddhist ideal that all should aim for *Nibbana*.

> ...Buddhism is best viewed as comprising not one, but three separate if interlocking systems: two soteriological systems...and one nonsoteriological system. Since the latter is primarily concerned with protection from danger, I shall call it *apotropaic* Buddhism. The two soteriological systems may be called *nibbanic* and *kammatic* Buddhism, respectively. Since its major concern is with release from the Wheel [of life], or nirvana (*nibbana*), nibbanic Buddhism is an appropriate term for normative soteriological Buddhism. Nonnormative soteriological Buddhism, concerned with improving one's position on the Wheel by improving one's karma (*kamma*), is appropriately termed kammatic Buddhism.*

Most Buddhists may well be aware of nibbanic Buddhism (to use Spiro's terms), but for the present life, at least, they are more concerned to improve their human lot, and thus are followers of kammatic Buddhism. As such, they offer prayers to the gods, and even—in spite of pure Buddhist doctrine which would demonstrate its uselessness—to the Buddha. These prayers could be to ask for a safeguard, or release, from troubles, or even to ask for worldly goods. In some other life they will seek to achieve the *summum bonum*—*Nibbana*—but for now 'Each day has troubles enough of its own.'**

Anatta is probably one of the most abstruse of the Buddhist doctrines, and as such it is beyond the needs of most lay-Buddhists. Spiro's observations concerning Burmese Buddhism can be taken as an accurate example of popular belief:

> Most Burmese are unaware of the meaning of *anatta*. Most of those who know about and/or understand the concept are reluctant—indeed find it psychologically impossible—to face up to its consequences. To do so would undermine the very basis of their soteriological aspirations and render meaningless the renunciations entailed by Buddhist morality. Committed to kammatic salvation, they insist—normative Buddhism notwithstanding—on the existence of an enduring soul which, persisting from rebirth to rebirth, experiences the consequences of karmic retribution.***

In their everyday lives the lay-people should help to maintain the

*Spiro, p. 12.
**Matthew 6: 34 (NEB).
***Spiro, pp. 88-9.

members of the *Sangha* (order of *bhikkhus*). This may be done in several ways, the most obvious being the giving of food to those *bhikkhus* who come to the village or town on their alms-round. Sometimes, as in Sri Lanka, it is the lay-people who go to the monastery to take the food there. This practice of giving food to the *bhikkhus* is a way for anyone to earn for himself (or herself) merit, thus improving his chances of a better rebirth. It is for this reason that it is the one who *gives* the food who expresses gratitude, and not the *bhikkhu* who receives it!

I hold the opinion that a surprising amount of information concerning the beliefs and practices of lay-Buddhists can be gleaned from a study of the various festivals and rituals that are carried out. I mention the following as examples:

(1) *Magha Puja*: Celebration of the giving of the code of rules (*Vinaya*) by which the *bhikkhus* live.
(2) *Vesakha* (Wesak): Celebration of the birth, enlightenment and death (attaining of *Nibbana*) of the Buddha, occurring in the month of May.
(3) *Vassa* (Buddhist 'Lent'): A time of year, approximately July to October, when *bhikkhus*, because it is the rainy season, stay in retreat in the monasteries; and some lay-folk may temporarily join the *Sangha* (order of *bhikkhus*) just for this period.
(4) *Hana Matsuri*: Japanese flower festival celebrating the birth of the Buddha.
(5) *Uposattha days*: There are four of these each lunar month, their times being dictated by the four quarter-phases of the moon.
(6) *Kataragama Festival*: This is a festival unique to Sri Lanka. You may well find that it is difficult to gain information on this subject, which I personally have found to be a fascinating one. If you can obtain a copy of *Buddhism: Beliefs and Practices in Sri Lanka* by L. A. de Silva (Sri Lanka, 1974), you will find a wealth of information both on this festival and on others.

For those teachers who wish to glean more details concerning contemporary lay-Buddhist practices, I have given details of three books in the bibliography which should prove particularly useful, if you are able to obtain them (and even afford them)—namely, those by Gombrich, King and Spiro. For those of you who have less time (or ambition!), I recommend the books by Ling, Naylor and Pye which are mentioned in the paragraph *after* the bibliography.

I have said it before, and I shall say it again for emphasis, there really is a dearth of readily available material on contemporary lay-Buddhism. If some kindly soul (not really a word to use in an article on Buddhism!) could write a book on such a subject, I am sure that he (or she) will earn great merit thereby!

BIBLIOGRAPHY

The books marked with an asterisk (*) are those which can be gainfully employed in laying a foundation course. This is not to say, however, that all the rest are technical. It is merely that the asterisked books are probably more easily obtainable. One further point: the publication dates are of those books which I have in my possession. Since I bought them, new and even revised editions may have been printed.

*W. T. de Bary (ed.), *The Buddhist Tradition* (*in India, China and Japan*) (New York, 1972). An anthology of texts.

*S. G. F. Brandon (ed.), *A Dictionary of Comparative Religion* (London, 1970).

K. K. S. Ch'en, *Buddhism in China* (Princeton, 1964).

*E. Conze, *Buddhism* (London, 1957).

—, *Buddhist Thought in India* (London, 1962).

S. Dutt, *The Buddha and Five After-Centuries* (London, 1957).

R. A. Gard, *Buddhism* (New York, 1963).

*H. von Glasenapp, *Buddhism—a Non-Theistic Religion* (London, 1970).

R. F. Gombrich, *Precept and Practice: Traditional Buddhism in the Rural Highlands of Ceylon* (Oxford, 1971).

L. A. Govinda, *The Psychological Attitude of Early Buddhist Philosophy: and Its Systematic Representation According to Abhidhamma Tradition* (London, 1961).

*I. B. Horner (trans.), *Milinda's Questions*, vols I and II (Sacred Books of the Buddhists, vols XXII-XXIII) (London, 1969). The Pali Text Society, of which Miss Horner is President, can provide a booklet listing numerous books from the Theravada Canon available in both Pali and English. Write to: Kegan Paul, Trench, Trubner Ltd, Bookstore 39, 39 Store Street, London WC1E 7DD.

*Winston L. King, *In the Hope of Nibbana* (La Salle, 1964).

*T. O. Ling, *A History of Religion East and West* (London, 1968). A useful book for placing Buddhism in contemporary contexts with other religious developments.

—, *The Buddha* (London, 1973).

Nyanaponika Thera, *The Heart of Buddhist Meditation* (London, 1969).

Nyanatiloka Thera, *Buddhist Dictionary. Manual of Buddhist Terms and Doctrines* (Colombo, 1956).

P. A. Pardue, *Buddhism* (New York/London, 1971).

*G. Parrinder (ed.), *Man and His Gods. Encyclopedia of the World's Religions* (London, 1973).

*Piyadassi Thera, *The Buddha's Ancient Path* (London, 1964).

*Walpola Rahula, *What the Buddha Taught* (Bedford, 1967).

R. H. Robinson, *The Buddhist Religion* (Belmont, Calif., 1970).
H. Saddhatissa, *The Buddha's Way* (London, 1971).
M. E. Spiro, *Buddhism and Society. A Great Tradition and Its Burmese Vicissitudes* (London, 1971).
*D. T. Suzuki, *An Introduction to Zen Buddhism* (London, 1972).
E. J. Thomas, *The Life of the Buddha* (reprinting).
—, *The History of Buddhist Thought* (London, 1951).
A. K. Warder, *Indian Buddhism* (Delhi, 1970).
*R. C. Zaehner (ed.), *The Concise Encyclopaedia of Living Faiths* (London, 1959).
*E. Zürcher, *Buddhism* (London, 1962).

Below 'A' level, the only adequate classroom books that I can suggest would be: T. O. Ling, *Buddhism* (Ward Lock Living Religion Series); David Naylor, *Thinking about Buddhism* (Lutterworth Educational); Michael Pye, *Zen and Modern Japanese Religions* (Ward Lock Living Religion Series); and the relevant chapter in B. W. Sherratt and D. J. Hawkins, *Gods and Men* (Blackie). If anyone comes across F. W. Rawding, *The Buddha* (Cambridge University Press), I suggest that this book should be used with great caution, since, for example, the Four Noble Truths given on page 32 are incorrect and Hinduism as depicted did not exist either by that name or in that form for many centuries! I most vehemently do *not* suggest C. A. Burland, *The Way of the Buddha* (Hulton Educational Publications).

For 'A' level, an intelligent selection from the books mentioned in the major list given above would be more than adequate.

Audio Visual Aids
Buddhism—World's Greatest Religions II (290), Life.
Encounter with Buddhism (F245, 29 frames), BBC Radiovision.
Buddhism (with taped commentary) (FF262, 65 frames), Concordia.
Buddhism (C6590, 30 frames), Educational Productions.
Life of Buddha, Hulton Educational.

Chapter 11

Teaching about Marxism

Controversial questions concerning the place, if any, of Marxism within a programme of religious education group themselves around five main areas:

(1) The over-all aim of religious education in schools.
(2) The strategies to be employed in the achievements of these aims.
(3) Definitions of religion and their relationship to Marxism as an ideology.
(4) The methodologies to be employed in the investigation.
(5) The selection and balancing of the aspects of Marxism to be examined, if it finds a place in the RE curriculum.

It is important to emphasise at the outset that the question of *aims* is primary and that the remaining questions, however important, are secondary. Hence, if certain assumptions are made—e.g., that it is in the aim of RE to convert pupils to a particular brand of Christianity and to initiate them into the worshipping community of that church— then a study of Marxism is unlikely to find a place unless as a target for criticism. Much of the confusion surrounding recent press discussion has arisen on account of unexamined and undefended pre-suppositions about aims.

An examination of the aims of RE is beyond the scope of this essay; the reader is referred to recent literature on the subject.* This essay proceeds on the value judgement that 'confession' aims are inappropriate in a pluralist society and that an open exploration of selected key commitments and life-styles is part of a balanced education. The word 'open' in this context does not preclude commitment.

Once aims are determined, arguments for and against the inclusion of Marxism begin to centre on questions of strategy—i.e., will the inclusion of Marxism be a potent factor in achieving the aims? Clearly, there is no one optimum content and it will be a question of choice. Today's religious educator finds himself living through an

*See, for example, I. Birnie (ed.), *Schools Council Working Paper 36* (Evans/ Methuen, 1971); *Religious Education and Integrated Studies* (article by Edwin Cox on aims) (SCM, 1972).

unprecedented explosion of knowledge. The dangerous consequence of this is that RE can begin to look like a great supermarket where the bewildered customer is invited to 'pick and mix' from a large variety of goods. The pitfalls are very real and there is an urgent need to establish criteria for selecting appropriate content.

Blackham, in arguing for the comparative study of religion in schools, says, 'Christian concepts, and many that are current in secular society, cannot be appreciated nor criticised nor firmly held until seen in the light of alternatives.'* It is the notion of contrasts which makes Marxism an attractive proposition for the open religious educator, the lifeblood of whose work is informed controversy rather than passive conformity. In his task of scrutinising implicit and explicit stances for living he will wish to lay bare a limited number of alternative visions of the goals of human existence. Marxism embodies a mode of coping with the human predicament and a vision of a new civilisation embraced in a variety of forms by approximately half of the world's population in the Soviet Union, China, Eastern Europe, Africa, South America and Western Europe. On these grounds, Marxism begins at least to rank high in the order of priorities. The contrasts should aid the understanding of Christian claims as well as exposing culturally determined presuppositions. This exercise should, at the same time, contribute to the vital task of education for world understanding. The mere fact that Marxism is an attractive proposition on these grounds for the RE teacher is not sufficient to carry the argument through. Few would wish to allow children to leave school ignorant about Marxism, but is the RE period the appropriate place?

At the practical level the arguments against it are reasonably strong. Many schools still only allow one period per week, and the training and presuppositions of many RE teachers make adequate and accurate coverage unlikely. The development of the new approach to RE, however, cannot be circumscribed by current limitations in the system; sound theoretical arguments need to be formulated as a basis for changing practice. It is at this point that questions about the definition of religion need to be examined.

It is interesting to note at the outset that it is frequently questioned whether Theravada Buddhism comes within the definition of religion, because it does not require assent to theism or belief in a soul. Is belief in a personal God and creator a necessary condition, or can transcendence be conceived in other ways? Several writers** have argued that

*H. J. Blackham, 'A Humanist Approach', in J. R. Hinnells (ed.), *Comparative Religion in Education* (Oriel, 1970), p. 56.
**See especially T. Ling, *Buddha, Marx and God* (Macmillan, 1966); N. Smart, *Mao* (Fontana, 1974).

Marxism contains within it all the dimensions which characterise religion. Ling's thesis* that religions were in origin total civilisations embodying guide-lines for a total way of life both public and private is an attractive one. The fact that religion in the West has come to be regarded as mainly concerned with man's private life may be seen to prejudice our view of religion and make for a definition which is too narrow. A decision on the issue of definition depends on which of the dimensions of religion are seen as crucial, and there can thus be no clear decision. It is sufficient for the purposes of this argument to point out some salient features which will at least put Marxism within the orbit of the religious educator who espouses the aim of scrutinising the most significant kinds of commitment likely to impinge upon his pupils' consciousness. These features have been summarised by Ling as follows:

> ... certain features of Marxism which seem to characterise it as a religion must be noticed. Besides the strongly eschatological nature of its doctrine, the evangelistic fervour of its adherents, their readiness for sacrificial action, and their sense of being in possession of an absolute and exclusive truth, there are such features as the prestige and authority which attaches to the writings of Marx, Engels and Lenin, an authority like that of sacred scripture.... Again, there is the veneration of the founders of communism ... the role of Moscow as the holy city, and the Politburo as the guardian of orthodoxy ... the quality of a conversion experience that often attaches to becoming a Marxist.**

The argument that the inclusion of Marxism transforms religious education into political education can to some extent be countered by this kind of analysis, but a more important point is that, unlike the Conservative or Labour parties, Marxism explicitly claims to discredit religion and to provide a substitute. From this position it can hardly expect to evade the scrutiny of the religious educator, though the latter will not provide the only angle of vision.

In so far as Marxism embodies to a greater or lesser extent the various dimensions of religion it follows that the methodologies to be employed in its exploration should be similar to those applied to religion.

Sharpe,*** in discussing 'comparative religion' and its methods, argues:

*T. Ling, *The Buddha* (Temple Smith, 1973).
**Ling, *Buddha, Marx and God*. See also Smart, *Mao*, for an analysis of Mao as a religious leader.
***N. Smart and D. Horder (eds.), *New Movements in Religious Education* (Temple Smith, 1975).

We are studying existential, intellectual, social and ethical
questions, rational and irrational, conscious and unconscious
attitudes, the spontaneous and the institutional together, in reaction
and interplay and there is no one instrument (save perhaps the
trained mind) sufficiently sensitive to be able to measure, weigh
and balance these and other factors singly and in combination. . . .
It might be argued that the complexities of methodology in comparative religion correspond very closely indeed to the complexity
of the phenomenon which is being studied.*

As in many other areas of his work the RE teacher will wish to co-
operate with and delegate various aspects of his work to colleagues in
other disciplines. His special contribution will consist in the gathering
together of the other angles of vision in order to provide a comprehensive understanding of them. This will be his distinctive
contribution and it arises on account of his operating in what Phenix*
describes as the 'synoptic' realm of meaning. Thus, for example, he
will consider key concepts such as materialism, alienation and
collectivism and key areas such as ethics and eschatology in the total
context of the underlying doctrine of man and vision of the goals of
human existence. In an educational setting this will best be done in a
comparative way.

The task of selecting aspects of Marxism to be considered is
particularly important because it is closely tied to achieving the degree
of objectivity which is required of the professional teacher. Thus, for
example, to deal only with Marx the prophet would lack balance
without some account of the subsequent developments seen in
historical perspective. Similarly, an examination of the resultant life-
styles in countries which worked out his ideas is a necessary ingredient.
Dr Krejci's article is included here in order to suggest a possible
balance by including the following elements:

(1) The social and intellectual background to Karl Marx.
(2) Marx's synthesis and message.
(3) Historical developments: reformist and revolutionary Marxism.
(4) Comments on life-styles in selected Communist countries.

It will readily be seen that many of the key concepts of Marxism are
beyond the grasp of any but the more able students of the fifth and
sixth forms. The same, however, could be said about a great deal of
the subject-matter of religious studies. The recommendations made
for a descriptive approach to other religions apply equally to

*P. H. Phenix, *Realms of Meaning* (McGraw-Hill, 1964).

Marxism. Thus, for example, a descriptive approach to the background in the nineteenth century and a treatment of Marx's response can be dealt with in the same way as with other famous men and women. There is much to recommend the treatment of the historical developments of Marxism through key figures like Lenin, Stalin and Mao. Where ideas are embodied in people they are more likely to evoke a response. Life-styles can be approached in a similar way by examining the day-to-day life of a contemporary student in, say, Russia or China.

A treatment of Marxism in the way suggested here is no more dangerous than a similar treatment of Christianity. The greater danger would be to allow pupils to leave school ignorant of these potent forces in the world. A commitment to objectivity and true professionalism on the part of the teacher is a basic requirement of any teacher of any subject. In religious studies it is particularly important because there is more at stake. It would be misleading, however, not to admit that the handling of potent forces like Christianity, Buddhism and Marxism is like poking crocodiles; there is always the possibility of someone getting bitten.

Resources

A comprehensive list of resources can be found in *Living Together*, City of Birmingham Handbook for RE. The following are selected in the light of the approach recommended in this chapter. The books listed are mostly appropriate to both teachers and pupils and take account of limited budgets and limited time.

(1) Background
L. F. Hobley, *Working Class and Democratic Movements* (Blackie, 1970).
Jackdaw Folders No. 7, *Shaftesbury and the Working Children*.
　　　　　　　No. 35, *The Early Trade Unions*.
　　　　　　　No. 95, *Charles Dickens*.
(2) Marx
A. Kettle, *Karl Marx* (Weidenfeld & Nicolson, 1968).
C. Seaward, *Karl Marx* (Wayland, 1974).
(3) Historical Developments and Key Figures
J. Charnock, *Red Revolutionary* (Methuen, 1968).
Jackdaw Folders No. 42, *The Russian Revolution*.
J. Lawrence, *A History of Russia* (Mentor, 1969).
I. E. Levine, *Lenin—The Man Who Made a Revolution* (Bailey Bros, 1970).
D. W. Mack, *Lenin and the Russian Revolution* (Longman, 1971).
K. Savage, *Marxism and Communism* (Bodley Head, 1968).
S. R. Schram, *Lenin* (Penguin, 1969).
—, *Mao Tse-tung* (Penguin, 1970).
N. Smart, *Mao* (Fontana, 1974).
C. Wright Mills, *The Marxists* (Pelican, 1962).

(4) Life-Styles and Other General Topics
U. Bronfenbrenner, *Two Worlds of Childhood* (Allen & Unwin, 1971).
L. Edwards, *Russia and Her Neighbours* (OUP, 1968).
N. Grant, *Soviet Education* (Pelican, 1968).
D. Hyde, *Communism Today* (Gill & Macmillan, 1972).
P. Lane, *Revolution* (Batsford, 1973).
J. Miller, *Life in Russia Today* (Batsford, 1969).
J. Popeson, *Let's Visit the USSR* (Burke, 1972).
R. Shepherd and R. Langley (eds.), *China* CEM Probe No. 18 (1974).
Solzhenitsyn's novels can be used for selecting material which highlights current moral and spiritual issues.

Sources of Information and Visual Aids for Teachers
The following agencies supply material:
Educational and Television Films Limited, 2, Doughty Street, London WC1N 2PJL.
The Society for Cultural Relations with the USSR, 320, Brixton Road, London SW9 6AB.
The Society for Anglo-Chinese Understanding, 24, Warren Street, London W1.
Central Books Ltd, 37, Grays Inn Road, London WC1X 8PS.

Films
BBC Television Enterprises Film Hire (25, The Burroughs, Hendon, London NW4) include the following films in their current catalogues:
Lenin's Revolution
Stalin's Revolution
Krushchev and the Thaw
From War to Revolution
The New China
The Revolution Will Not Now Take Place

MARXISM

(1) Background
Marx's ideas and their impact on intellectual and political development in the world cannot be understood without reference to the sources which provided some of the corner-stones of his social philosophy (see Scheme 1).

Karl Marx (1818-83) spent his life in Germany (Trier, Bonn, Berlin and Cologne), France (Paris), Belgium (Brussels) and, above all, England (London). He lived during a period of intensified secularisation and industrialisation of European society, and in that part of Europe which was most affected by these processes.

In his lifetime the belief in established religion became weakened by the spread of scepticism connected with the rapid developments in the scientific field. The advance of science gave rise to a new and very efficient technology. This, however, would not have been possible without the growing interest in enterprising activity in the economic sphere. The enterprising spirit and the fast-developing technology resulted in an unprecedented growth of productivity. As this required a considerable amount of money for investment, profit became essential for industrialisation. This, however, was pushed beyond socially justified limits.

The quest for higher productivity everywhere released the labour force from agriculture and brought it into the towns and industrial centres. A corollary of the developing technology was growing public hygiene. Although medical care for the poor was either inadequate or non-existent, the devastating epidemics at least were stopped, and there was unprecedented population-increase. The labour force was bountiful and cheap. These conditions were exploited by the entrepreneurs who, unchecked by considerations of social consciousness, thought rather in terms of newly discovered economic principles of supply and demand and paid most of the workers wages far below the subsistence level.

The working conditions in the newly rising industries were appalling: at least a twelve-hour working day, women working in most difficult jobs such as in mines, and even children (from the age of 10 or even younger) working in factories. It is no wonder that criticism spread; some of it was carried on the basis of awakened religious consciousness, but a new and, as it later appeared, more efficient criticism was voiced by those who tried to understand the functioning of the industrialised society and find a way of abolishing the merciless exploitation of those who could not earn their livelihood other than by selling their labour.

Against this background the development of three ways of thought has to be understood. Religious explanation of man's predicament and the development of mankind was challenged by philosophical, metaphysical speculation on this topic. Most of this speculation came from Germany, the country of Marx's birth. There was a series of prominent philosophers who influenced the development of thought throughout the world. Yet one among them concentrated mainly on the theory of human and social development and was best suited to the quest for the possible change of social conditions. This was Hegel (1770-1831).

On the other hand, interest in operating the newly born economic system resulted in the rise of a new scientific discipline, the so-called political economy. Its founding fathers were Adam Smith (1723-90) and Ricardo (1772-1823) in England.

Finally, criticisms of social evils resulting from the newly rising economic conditions were most consistently voiced by thinkers who eventually became called Socialists or, as Marx's followers prefer to say, Utopian Socialists. The most prominent among them were Saint-Simon (1760-1825) and Fourrier (1772-1837) in France.

SCHEME ONE
BACKGROUND AND SOURCES

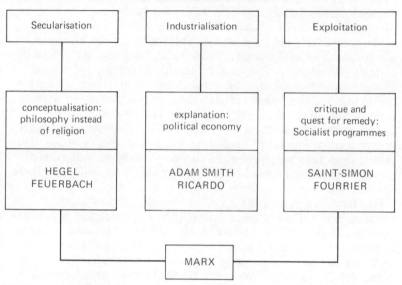

Secularisation	Industrialisation	Exploitation
conceptualisation: philosophy instead of religion	explanation: political economy	critique and quest for remedy: Socialist programmes
HEGEL FEUERBACH	ADAM SMITH RICARDO	SAINT-SIMON FOURRIER

MARX

(2) Marx's Synthesis and Message

Karl Marx became well acquainted with all three aforementioned schools of thought: with the German, especially Hegelian, philosophy; with the English political economy; and with the French Socialist blueprints. His creative contribution was in amalgamating all these three elements into one more or less coherent theory or, rather, philosophy, which he then further developed during his lifetime.

In his youth, while still in Germany, Marx was most impressed by the Hegelian philosophy of dialectics, but he could not accept Hegel's idealistic and, in a way, religious position. He followed, rather, the anti-religious, materialistic line of Feuerbach (1804-72). So Marx eventually put forward his own concept of dialectical materialism, of which the basic concepts can be seen to contain two basic principles.

First, the world is matter, moving in conformity to law; our knowledge, being the highest product of nature, is in a position to reflect this conformity to law. Increasing conformity to this law means a greater knowledge and command over nature and consequently human freedom. The criterion of our correct cognition and, therefore, of truth is that our ideas coincide with that objective reality which exists independently of ourselves.

Secondly, the movement of matter occurs in a dialectical way (this has been taken over from Hegel)—i.e., in a three-stage rhythm of thesis, anti-thesis (opposition) and synthesis. Transition from one stage to another occurs when the continuous and gradual quantitative change becomes a qualitative one. When this happens it is a comparatively sudden, leap-like change.

Marx, however, was interested in philosophy not for its own sake, but for that of social change. As he put it, he could not follow the path of philosophers who only explained the world; he wanted to change it. In applying the dialectical materialism to social development, Marx suggested also that the changes in the development of humanity take place in a three-phase rhythm.

To a given scope and level of production forces (technology) corresponds a certain mode of production (socio-economic system). This position can best be described as thesis. As soon as the productive forces outgrow the established mode of production (antithesis), there is a need for another mode of production (synthesis).

In Marx's view, adaptation of the mode of production to the productive forces takes place through the class struggle which has been the essence of the history of all societies. The class struggles culminate in revolutions which achieve sudden, qualitative changes necessary to adapt the mode of production to the productive forces.

In Marx's view, previous social revolutions have resulted in replacing the old ruling class with a new one, more efficient, but in principle equally exploitative. The reason was that those who worked did not dispose of the product of their labour. This was largely appropriated as profits, rents or interest by those who owned the means of production, whether this was land, cattle, workshops, raw materials, engines or just financial assets used in production.

In the course of European history, according to Marx, three modes of production or socio-economic formation followed each other. The slave-holding mode of production was followed by feudalism and this, since about the sixteenth to eighteenth centuries, has been replaced by the capitalist mode of production. Before the dawn of history, humanity lived in a stage of primitive communism not divided into classes. The classless society is also a future prospect, though on a higher level of knowledge and technology. The development of humanity has attained a stage where the basic contradiction is between the capitalist and the proletarian (a free but exploited and alienated being). The proletarians have the opportunity to make a revolution, a socialist revolution, which in nationalising private ownership will abolish classes and therewith connected exploitation and alienation.

Both these terms acquired, in Marx's thought, specific meaning. In his early writings Marx developed the concept of alienation. He took it from Hegel, but gave it another context. Whereas Hegel talked of man's alienation from God, Marx conceived it as man's alienation from his society because of the appalling conditions of his existence in it. He realised that those who had to perform day-long hard manual work from early childhood could not derive any satisfaction either from their work or in their family lives or from their leisure-time, which was virtually non-existent. He saw in this multiple alienation the main vice of the socio-economic formation, which he labelled 'capitalism'.

Later, Marx devoted his main voluminous work to the analysis of the capitalist mode of production in which he tackled the issue of exploitation. Marx accepted Ricardo's labour theory of value, according to which products are priced according to the amount of labour spent on their fabrication. But he disagreed with Ricardo's acceptance of the relative rewards of labour, land and capital as legitimate rewards of factors of production. As Marx saw in the labour the only source of value, he conceived profits, rents and interest as surplus value. The ratio of this surplus value to the sum of wages Marx considered as the rate of exploitation.

As was said earlier, however, Marx did not wish only to explain; he desired to change the social condition. Therefore, he devoted most of his energy to political activity. In Paris he came across Socialist circles, in London he got in touch with the emerging trade unions and with the impressive Chartist Movement. He tried to co-ordinate and influence all these groups and organisations on an international scale.

In all his work, theoretical and practical, Marx was helped most by his close associate, Friedrich Engels (1820-95), who after Marx's death became the head of the Marxian school of thought.

Marx and Engels tried to build up an active revolutionary force, first in the League of the Communists, then in the so-called First International (1864-76). Yet there were also other views on how to build a more equal and just society: there were, on the one hand, those represented mainly by a Russian revolutionary, Bakunin (1814-76); on the other hand, different, rather reformist, streams within the labour movement. The latter considered the main task to be a gradual but tangible improvement of the workers' position with a simultaneous expansion of democratic rights. The German Social Democrat leader Lassalle (1825-64) was one of these. When in 1889 the so-called Second or Socialist International was founded, the reformists in it won the upper hand. This International became an association of Socialist and Labour parties with both Marxist and non-Marxist orientation.

(3)   Two Faces of Marxian Heritage
After Engels' death, three main alternative ways of developing the
Marxian heritage emerged (see Scheme 2). On one side there were
those who considered Marx's contribution crucial but not infallible.
They looked upon it as a theory which, as a scientific theory, has
continuously to be improved and, if necessary, revised. The most
prominent representative of this view was Eduard Bernstein (1850-
1932).

The other stream wished to stick as far as possible to Marx's
bequest; when a new problem arose, the question was 'What would
Marx's position have been?' The main promoter of this way of
thinking was Karl Kautsky (1854-1938).

Both Bernstein and Kautsky, however, met on the practical plane of
their respective interpretations. They both stood for a rather non-
violent transformation of society, within the expanding framework of
parliamentary democracy and civil liberties.

The third stream wished to bring Marx's teaching to its radical
conclusions, to promote a socialist revolution which would expro-
priate the private owners of the means of production and establish the
dictatorship of the proletariat in order to abolish social inequalities.
This stream was represented by the Russian revolutionary, Lenin
(1870-1924), founder of a tightly knit and disciplined Communist
Party. This organisation proved most efficient in the chaotic situation
which developed in Russia towards the end of the Second World War.
After a two-fold revolution (1917) and civil war (1918-21) Lenin's
Communist Party won dictatorial power (so-called dictatorship of
proletariat) and transformed Russia into the Union of Soviet Socialist
Republics.

On the other hand, in other European countries it was rather the
reformist socialism which prevailed. Universal suffrage, social
insurance, labour legislation and the wage-bargaining power of trade
unions were its main practical achievements. Social democratic parties
continued to be members of the Second International, which also
encompassed the non-Marxist Socialist and Labour parties. The
Second International has survived until today. Communist parties,
organised according to the Soviet Russian example, became united in
the Communist, or the Third, International (1919-43).

(4) Lenin's Heritage
After Lenin's death (1924) there was a struggle for leadership and also
for the manner in which Socialism had to develop. Stalin (1879-1953)
emerged as the most powerful, and considered himself the legitimate
heir of Lenin and consequently the only correct interpreter of what has
now become described as Marxism-Leninism. One of its main

SCHEME TWO
REFORMIST AND REVOLUTIONARY MARXISM

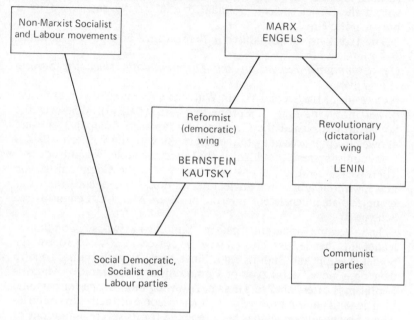

principles was the assumption that the USSR is the fatherland of Socialism and the Communist parties the vanguard of the proletariat. The following points were stressed in Marx's and Engels' writings: The transformation of the society will be achieved in two stages. First, the Socialist stage, in which social differences and even classes will still survive but these classes and also their contradictions will not be antagonistic (contradictory); and everyone will be rewarded according to his merits. Second, the Communist stage, when everyone will receive according to his needs, when antagonism within society will be abolished and when everybody will realise his freedom within the framework of scientifically recognised necessity. To achieve this glorious aim, unselfish work for the community and eager fulfilment of the tasks and targets put forward by the political leadership are required.

Stalin not only won dictatorial power in the Communist Party of Soviet Russia, but he also physically liquidated his rivals. Trotsky (1879-1940), for example, who disagreed with Stalin mainly in international matters and stood for world socialist revolution as against Stalin's policy of building socialism in one country, the USSR, was exiled. After eleven years in exile Trotsky was assassinated. His followers (Trotskyists) criticised Stalin not only because of his ruthlessness, but also because of the new inequalities which emerged within the Soviet society, dominated and strictly supervised by a bureaucratic élite.

The Trotskyists are organised in the so-called Fourth International.

(5) *Communist Expansion and Differentiation since the Second World War*

As a result of the Second World War, the Communists won exclusive power in a wide area of Europe and Asia (1945-9). Wherever the Soviet armies ousted the German and Japanese occupants or were allowed to enter according to the agreement with the Western Allies, a Communist system, moulded on the Soviet example, was introduced. There were, however, a few countries where the Communists won power without substantial Soviet intervention. Consequently there was scope for an independent interpretation of Marxism-Leninism (see Scheme 3).

This became apparent first in Yugoslavia, whose Communist leadership, headed by Tito (1892-   ), ceased in 1948 to follow the Soviet example and Stalin's lead. Since then, Yugoslavia has tried to develop a more liberal type of Communism. Her brand of Marxist-Leninism is often labelled Titoism. Allowing more scope for personal liberties and national sovereignty, it has become attractive to countries where Soviet supremacy has been resented for its severe limitations of personal liberties and/or for nationalistic reasons.

China is the other country where Communists won power without direct Soviet intervention. At first, China followed the example of the USSR. After Stalin's death, however, divergencies became apparent, which eventually led to Mao Tse-Tung (1893-1976) assuming the role of the authoritative interpreter of the Marxist-Leninist heritage for the under-developed countries, the so-called Third World. Here the peasantry rather than the industrial proletariat provides the backbone of the revolutionary movement. The Maoist attitude has been strengthened by the different interests of China and the USSR as nations. Also the different cultural traditions influenced the diverging roads of Russian and Chinese Marxism.

So it happened that, where Marxism-Leninism became the dominant teaching, it was sub-divided into three main streams; each of them is based on a sovereign state—the USSR, China and Yugoslavia. Whereas the Chinese version can be described as Maoist, the Yugoslav version as Titoist, that of the USSR can best be described as that of the Soviet Establishment. Most European Communist-ruled countries are allied with the USSR (Warsaw Pact), and more or less follow her internal policy as well (Bulgaria,

SCHEME THREE
MARXISM—LENINISM

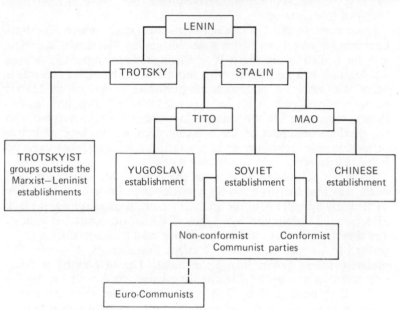

Czechoslovakia, Hungary, East Germany and Poland). Yet Romania, which is also a member of that alliance, follows, in international relationships at least (significantly not in internal matters), rather the Titoist pattern. Other Communist parties in the Soviet-led bloc who wished to develop their own reformed and more liberal type of Communism (Hungary 1956, Czechoslovakia 1968) were prevented from doing so by Soviet armed intervention. On the other hand, Polish Communists succeeded in striking a certain precarious compromise between Soviet requirements of uniformity and more scope for the citizens' self-assertion.

Albania is a special case in Europe; sheltered by Yugoslavia from direct contact with the Soviet allies, she became a dedicated ally of China and follows rather the Maoist path. On the other hand, Communist countries such as North Korea and Vietnam try to keep a precarious balance between the two Communist super-powers, the USSR and China. In their internal policies they represent a very rigid type of Communism. Mongolia, land-locked between China and the USSR, is in all aspects (both internal and external policies) closely related to the USSR. Cuba turned to Marxism-Leninism only after the revolutionaries under Fidel Castro won power (1959). Although economically dependent on the Soviet bloc, Cuba managed, because of her geographical position, to develop her own, more nation-bound brand of Communism.

In contrast to the Communist-dominated states where Marxism-Leninism became the exclusive state philosophy, Marxism in the West and partly also in the Third World is interpreted, especially among intellectuals, in a non-conformist, more or less liberal, way. Stress is being laid more on philosophical principles conceived in Marx's earlier writings, such as for instance the theory of alienation. In this theory, the young Marx considered not only the economic, but also the psychic conditions of the working class within an exploitative socio-economic system (mode of production), and laid more stress on individual freedom than in his later writings.

From this point of view, some of the Western Marxists are critical of the way that socialism has been developed in Eastern Europe; they particularly disapprove of the Stalinist terror, the inequalities, the lack of personal freedom and new types of alienation connected with it. Yet they believe that in their respective countries socialism can be realised in a better way. Some Western Communists, however, still prefer to follow Soviet Russia's example. The new mood is being reflected in a number of Communist parties, most explicitly by the Italian Communists. They first ceased to consider exclusive power (dictatorship) a necessary precondition of the way to socialism. Italian Marxists also have their own rather independent theoreticians such as Gramsci (1897-1937) and Togliatti (1893-1964). Recently, the Communist parties which have declared their willingness to abide by democratic pluralism, to respect human rights and participate in an integrated Western Europe became labelled Euro-Communists.

(6) Life under the Marxist-Leninist Establishment

Wherever Communists took exclusive power, and consequently Marxism-Leninism became the state philosophy, there were considerable changes in the life-style. Although there are quite remarkable differences between individual Communist countries, they also have much in common. First there is the stress on education in the Marxist-Leninist world view. This excludes as a matter of principle any religious beliefs and practices. The general tendency is to tolerate religious practices in the adult population, but to exclude them from vital sectors of the society such as the civil service, police and education at all levels and thereby to prevent it from influencing youth. China and Soviet Russia both follow this line very vigorously. In Russia, people under 18 are not allowed to attend religious services. Moreover, only duly registered services can take place legally. In Poland, on the other hand, where there is a strong Catholic Church and Catholic tradition which are considered integral parts of the national heritage, there is remarkable tolerance towards religion: although religious education is also officially discouraged, it is not made as difficult as in other Communist countries.

Another particular feature of the life-style in the Communist countries is the stress on the individuals' responsibility and duty towards society. Freedom in the sense that everyone can do what he wants to is not understood as an individual prerogative. This, rather, is considered as licence; genuine freedom is seen in behaviour corresponding to the needs of the society. So, in the Marxist-Leninist sense, freedom is based on correct cognition. It is supposed that Marxism-Leninism provides full understanding of the laws of social development and, therefore, also understanding of the needs of society in the individual stages of its development. Interpretation of social laws and evaluation of social needs are matters for the supreme bodies of the respective Communist parties in the Soviet bloc; ultimately of the Communist Party of the USSR. Everybody is supposed to follow the Party's lead and to contribute, as far as possible, to the fulfilment of the Party targets. Collective targets, and not individual interests, provide criteria for what individuals have to do (individual actions).

The differences between the individual Communist-dominated states are seen in the scope which is left to individuals' self-determination. In China there is not much left. In the drive to abolish all differences between manual and non-manual labour and differences between towns and countryside, the younger generation has to get acquainted with all types of work. Students of all disciplines have to spend some time (even several years) in production, mainly in the countryside, in order to acquire the common socialist consciousness of a working man. Consumer standards are widely equalised. The sense of austerity prevails.

In Soviet Russia there is no such equalisation. Income and living-standard differentials are considerable. Between towns and countryside a wide gap continues to prevail. All students have to acquire a solid knowledge of Marxism-Leninism (pass an examination) and prove their loyalty to the Party line. Additional work (the so-called voluntary brigades) for the general benefit is often required from most of the population. In particular, the teenagers are drawn through their schools to help at harvest time (hops, sugar beet, potatoes, etc.).

The position of the Soviet Establishment can best be shown by the Moral Code for the Builder of Communism, formulated at the 1961 Congress of the Communist Party of the USSR, which reads:

Devotion to the Communist cause, love of the Socialist motherland
and of the other Socialist countries;

Conscientious labour for the good of society—he who does not work,
neither shall he eat;

Concern on the part of everyone for the preservation and growth of
public wealth;

A high sense of public duty, intolerance of actions harmful to the
public interest;

Collectivism and comradely mutual assistance: one for all and all for
one;

Humane relations and mutual respect between individuals—man is to
man a friend, a comrade and brother;

Honesty and truthfulness, moral purity, modesty and guilelessness in
social and private life;

Mutual respect in the family, and concern for the upbringing of
children;

An uncompromising attitude to injustice, parasitism, dishonesty and
careerism;

Friendship and brotherhood among all peoples of the USSR, intolerance of national and racial hatred;

An uncompromising attitude to the enemies of Communism, peace
and the freedom of nations;

Fraternal solidarity with the working people of all countries, and with
all peoples.

(Translation by Donald Evans, *Communist Faith and Christian
Faith* (London, 1965), pp. 94-5.)

So Communists have their Twelve Commandments. The case is
similarly put forward by Mao Tse-tung:

A Communist should be frank, faithful and active, looking upon
the interests of the revolution as his very life and subordinating his
personal interests to those of the revolution; he should, always and
everywhere adhere to correct principles and wage a tireless struggle
against all incorrect ideas and actions, so as to consolidate the
collective life of the Party and strengthen the ties between the Party
and the masses; and he should be more concerned about the Party
and masses than about the individual and more concerned about
others than about himself. Only thus can he be considered a
communist. ('Combat Liberalism', in *Essential works of Marxism*,
ed. A. P. Mendel, Bantam Books, 1968.)

In contrast to the Soviet and Maoist establishment, the Yugoslav
type of Marxism-Leninism is less demanding on the individual.

Although here also the collective interests come first, the individual has greater scope for self-assertion. This happens not only in the economic sphere, where farms below ten hectares and small enterprises employing five or less persons are allowed, but also in cultural aspects. The Communist Party is also less rigidly organised. The individual states of the Yugoslav Federation have a much wider say in economic and, up to a point, cultural matters than do the individual republics of the USSR.

Finally, it has also to be mentioned that within the Soviet bloc there are quite wide differences in life-style. This depends mainly on the respective national tradition and on the level of cultural development. Another important element is the degree of rigidity of the political regime. At present this seems to be tightest in Soviet Russia and East Germany, then follows Czechoslovakia, Romania and Bulgaria. On the other hand, Poland and Hungary are trying to find a compromise between the Soviet line and the longing of their populations for more individual self-assertion.

On the whole, however, and with the aforementioned qualifications, the Marxist-Leninist establishment tends to concentrate political, economic and ideological power in one supreme body at the top. This gives it unprecedented scope for power over its subjects. Freedom to oppose the Government, to associate against its will, to propagate other than official views, to travel abroad or leave the country, to work or not to work, and other similar possibilities which in the West are taken for granted, are excluded, or at least severely limited, in the Communist states.

It is possible to trace a parallel between the demands made on an individual adherent by the state doctrine of Marxism-Leninism and the demand made by an intolerant religious orthodoxy. Criticism of the basic tenets of the doctrine is not allowed; in discussions it is often the appropriate quotation from Marx, Lenin or Mao, rather than empirical test, which decides the issue. Also the belief in a sequence of socio-economic formations, a sequence which eventually will end in an ideal type of society, reminds one of religious eschatology, because, although the final outcome is taken from heaven to earth, it nevertheless transcends the scope of a scientific forecast. Last, but not least, an elaborate ritual displayed especially on festive occasions such as the May Day parade, celebration of the Revolution Day, etc., assumes features which many observers and participants consider quasi-religious.

Understandably, the lack of individual liberties has evoked dissent. This has been strongest in countries of the Soviet establishment. In Soviet Russia only a few outstanding personalities, however, could voice their views. Most of them had to undergo prison penalties. Only the writer Solzhenitsyn (1918-) and the scientist Sakharov (1921-), the two most prominent Russian fighters for individual freedom, were subject to harassment rather than prosecution. Solzhenitsyn, however, had served a long prison sentence under Stalin. In Yugoslavia, the best-known critic of the Soviet and, in a way, also Yugoslav establishment is Djilas (1911-). However, the greatest mass support for liberalising tendencies has been in Poland, Hungary and Czechoslovakia. The 1968 Czechoslovakia reform movement aiming at 'Socialism with a human face' was an articulate expression of comprehensive reformist tendencies within the Marxist-Leninist establishment itself. The USSR leadership, however, is determined to nip in the bud any similar attempts.

Many countries with a Marxist-Leninist establishment made formal proclamations of individual liberties which, however, are contradicted by administrative practice. Most of the governments of these countries have signed an international agreement in Helsinki (1975) which, in order to diminish tensions between East and West, required, among other things, extension of individual civil and political liberties in all signatory countries. Yet there is strong reluctance to honour these declarations in practice. Because of this, audacious people in the countries concerned started to point out these discrepancies and ask the governments to behave according to the accepted principles. This moral, rather than political, opposition has been active for some time in the USSR and Poland and recently has gathered momentum in Czechoslovakia, where it has adopted the symbolic name of Charter 77.

Conclusion

This survey of the background, key ideas, historical development and current manifestations of Marxism has served to highlight the diverse nature of the phenomenon in a way which should discourage an over-simplified approach. The complex development will continue into the future, and one aspect of importance to ourselves and our pupils will be the continuing interaction between the different ideologies and social systems. In this encounter the well-informed are more likely to make a valid contribution to debate and decision and thereby help to create a more humane world.

Chapter 12

What About Christianity?

I have still some copies of an excellent chart which I used with my comprehensive-school classes to prove that Jesus really did rise from the dead. Teachers probably know it. Certain counter-solutions like 'the wrong tomb' or 'Jesus wasn't really dead' are put forward, but then the pupil is referred to such New Testament passages as Mark, 15:46 and 47, Luke, 23:55 and 56, or Mark, 15:42-5, to show that the early Church had already dealt with these objections. Even though I changed to discussing the significance of the Resurrection for Christians rather than trying to argue it as a historical fact, and so had stopped using the chart, it came as something of a surprise in 1968 when I first began to study Islam to discover that the Muslim faith denies the Crucifixion of Jesus and therefore, quite naturally, has no place for the Resurrection! No wonder some Christians are opposed to teaching about other religions in the classroom. They do pose threats, if the purpose of teaching is to induct pupils into a faith; consequently no rationale has yet been worked out for including world religions in the RE syllabuses of denominational schools which does not require at some point an assurance to be given of Christianity's superiority or else leaves the relationship open—unconsidered—a skeleton among the vestments.

In the county school the issue can be ducked. It is not part of the exercise to evaluate, to deal in absolute truth. Courses can stop short of this challenge or can dispassionately consider the possible relationship which may exist between the extreme positions of Christianity being true and the rest false, of them all being true, or of all of them being false. In the denominational school to which children are sent to be inducted into a particular faith—Judaism or Anglican or Roman Catholic Christianity—evasion would seem to be a shirking of responsibility, and the propagation of any view other than the finality of Christianity would appear to be betraying Jesus with a liberal kiss.

As someone whose teaching career has always been in the maintained sector of education, and as one concerned with the ultimate issues of dialogue and the relationships of one faith to another, but who must confess dissatisfaction with all the solutions, I do not feel qualified to answer the voluntary school's problems. Perhaps there is no completely satisfactory solution, but I think diocesan education committees drafting their syllabuses must give the matter serious attention.

This excursion has not been irrelevant if it has drawn attention to the embarrassment which the presence of articulate Islam or Humanism is to Christianity. When a gurdwara collects £77 as an instant response to an appeal from a Sikh social worker in Amritsar, or Muslims share in a street collection for Oxfam, we can no longer get away with the claim that only Christians care. When we know that for the Judaism of his day the crucifixion of Jesus was as much a non-event as apparently the destruction of the Temple was to his followers forty years later, we are bound to walk with care. The extravagant claims of former times can no longer be made.

Perhaps this embarrassment is one reason why the teaching of world religions has had little apparent effect on approaches to the teaching of Christianity. Tension and the problems of commitment have tended to leave it untouched. The two strands have certainly not become interwoven in courses on such topics as Jewish, Muslim and Christian beliefs about Jesus even in the sixth form where it might be possible and worthwhile, and contact has even been lacking in the area of methodology and aim. The Bible text, not the practised faith, is still the foundation stone of the Christianity syllabus, and the aim—what it means to be a Jew or Sikh in terms of practice and belief—has still to be applied to Christianity.

Besides embarrassment, there is the problem of familiarity in two forms. First, we know so much about Christianity—too much. We have to preface our teaching by 'ifs', and parenthesise it with 'buts', to an extent we do not find necessary with other faiths because we do not know them as fully. Consequently we become confused in aim. How Christians worship becomes a journey from the Catholic Mass to the Anglican Eucharist and the Quaker meeting with six or seven other halts on the way—and then there is Series Three as well as the Book of Common Prayer! We end up rubbing our sore feet, our minds far away from worship. Secondly, we know too much about the church on the corner. Many RE teachers have become disenchanted with it. It stands for gossip, waste of money and talent, and wrong priorities. So, in the same way, are the parents of our pupils, and therefore the pupils themselves, disaffected. 'What's the good of going to church?' they ask. Many teachers, when their hands are on their hearts, find it difficult to provide an answer. Christianity, unlike Sikhism or Judaism, can suffer because pupils and teachers know it at first or second hand and not merely in idealistic terms. Gurdwaras, mosques and synagogues are as open to criticism as churches, but most of us are unaware of the ways in which they fall short of their ideals.

To present Christianity as a world religion, to treat it as we do Islam or Judaism and Humanism but perhaps giving it more time because of its cultural importance, is not easy, but some re-appraisal is urgent.

THE REINSTATEMENT OF CHRISTIANITY IN
RELIGIOUS EDUCATION

Recent trends in thinking about religious education have resulted in what has been called 'Christless Christianity' and an anxiety among many committed Christian teachers of the subject. They have been made to feel that any reference to their personal beliefs is wrong and that the subject should now be left in the hands of agnostics or Humanists. Can a way forward be found which will be fair to Christianity and respectful to the Christian or non-Christian teacher and the uncommitted child, or to the pupil committed to the Christian faith or some other religion or to Humanism or Marxism?

Motive

To take the second issue first, one must point out that confessionalism, indoctrination (whatever dirty word one chooses to use), is a matter of motive and approach rather than of content. One may teach Christianity enthusiastically, interestingly and fairly (fair to the child and to the faith) and yet not be evangelistic. One may teach Islam or Buddhism, and certainly Humanism and Marxism, in such a way as to be guilty of Christian evangelism! If the Christian teacher is capable of acknowledging that other people find meaning through a commitment to Islam or Humanism, if he can share the humility expressed in the already quoted words of Max Warren ('Our first task in approaching another people, another culture, another religion, is to take off our shoes, for the place we are approaching is holy. Else we may find ourselves treading on men's dreams.'), he need not concern himself about a charge of being an evangelist; neither need he hide his own commitment.

Content

In terms of content there is, of course, a need to turn words into deeds. It is hollow to acknowledge that there are sincere and committed Jews or Humanists, and then ignore their beliefs in the classroom. For the Christian who cannot happily teach about them there seems to be three choices, the last more practical in a city like Leeds than in Malton or Dawlish. First, there may be a colleague who will teach the other aspects of the syllabus. In larger schools there is often more than one RE teacher, and division of content is sensible; no one can be a master of all trades. Secondly, there are now good aids to the teaching of Hinduism, Judaism, Buddhism, Islam and Sikhism, and a group of Humanists is attempting to provide materials for the study of that faith. If education is a partnership, the teacher should be able to assist his pupils to find out for themselves what Jews or Muslims do and believe. Finally, it may be possible to invite a Jew, a Sikh or a Humanist into school to share the work done under the second suggestion (not to give a 'one-night stand' to pupils totally ignorant of the faith) and to visit a synagogue or gurdwara. Of course, one cannot study every faith, but at least one should be examined—the one someone can help the pupils to study, perhaps the one locally represented.

Turning now to the Christian syllabus, two considerations need to be borne in mind. First, it should not be 'Christless'; secondly, it should be at least as interesting and comprehensive as a course on Judaism or Islam! This means it should be multi-dimensional rather than exclusively biblical. Put another way, the school-leaver has a right to know what it means to be a Christian in terms of practice, belief and commitment. Areas of study would include:

(1) The church as a building, leading from architecture, contents, and variety of shapes (cf. different denominations and periods) to worship.

(2) The Christian community of believers, (*a*) their belief in Jesus (Jesus the man, a Jew of his time, leading to the Jesus of faith), (*b*) as the body of Christians (their festivals and worship), (*c*) their divisions and movements with their varying emphases (including 'Youthquake' groups), (*d*) their social and missionary activities.

(3) Christianity and art, music and literature.

Warnings

A number of irrelevancies and ways to boredom are to be avoided. One is the over-indulgence in the history of church buildings. Architecture can be fascinating and can stimulate aesthetic appreciation, but Christianity is more than architecture, and churches are supposedly built to the glory of God. The study should lead to worship, the forms of worship, the use of hymns, prayers and the Bible in worship, and eventually to a consideration of the question 'What is worship?' The second danger is that of becoming absorbed in denominationalism. Liturgical variety may be interesting, and is important, but sectarianism is irrelevant now to all but a few Christians. Why ask children to share our foolishness? An endless journey from church to church can be as worthless as the third danger, the tedious discussion of Christian attitudes to sex, leisure, marriage, money, drugs, war, race, work and pollution. It would be much better to assist pupils to discover the distinctive criteria which Christians use in making moral decisions and choices, perhaps by finding out what prompted such people as Huddleston and Luther, Penn and Wilberforce to make their particular stands. But let us not forget that most Christians have never been pacifists, not all white South Africans agreed with Trevor Huddleston, and that Robert Owen, Charles Bradlaugh and Peter Hain, not to mention Gandhi and Muhammad, have also had their principles and have suffered for them. There must be no distortion of the truth by suggesting that only Christians care or that there is one agreed Christian view. There are Bible-Christians who accept divorce or abortion or who are teetotal or pacifist; there are others who take the opposite views. Does one possess the Spirit and the other not? If we wish our pupils to make some commitment to life, and not merely to be drifters, it seems wrong to present them with some non-existent brand of monolithic Christianity claiming this to be the only way of interpreting life, finding meaning in it and responding to it.

I have not attempted to programme this course from first school to sixth form—that is another exercise—but I would suggest that there is wisdom in beginning with the phenomena and proceeding from the church as a building and a place of worship, and Jesus as a man, and the Bible thought of in terms of scrolls, ancient writing and a book used in worship, towards the Body of Christ, the Jesus of faith, and biblical theology. In doing so, one should avoid giving the impression that there are two or more levels of Christian, those who require 'visual aids' or choruses, the beauty of holiness and sacramentalism, and those for whom meditation or abstract theology provide spiritual nourishment. Christians differ, but perhaps by now we have sufficient understanding of human psychology to know that for some the Quaker Meeting provides the awareness of the presence of God which another finds in the Mass and a third at a Billy Graham meeting, and that no one way is superior to the others, however preferable it may be to one personally!

Finally, thinking of examinations, I would look for a change from Bible knowledge to Christian knowledge, with candidates asked to answer not only what Jesus taught about the family or discipleship, but also what contribution Sydney Carter or J. S. Bach has made to religious music, to describe and explain the significance of a Christian act of worship which they have attended, or to explain why Christianity is a missionary religion.

The approach outlined above has its imperfections, and rejects the strictures of the 1944 Act, but it does represent an attempt to re-instate Christianity and to present it in such a way that a Muslim living in Britain or one of the indigenous products of our own secular society (ignorant of Christianity but hostile to it) will understand the culture which is still Christian-based and the faith which lies behind it. One hopes, for example, that he will know why Sunday, not Tuesday or even Saturday, is the 'odd' day of the week, and why we use holly,

Christmas trees and illuminations at Christmas. Instead of complaining about commercialism, teachers could (and many do) help children to understand the significance of the customs attached to Christian festivals. Through the tinsel it is possible to penetrate to the essential.

The 'world religions movement' and those who like myself would logically extend the scope of religious studies to include other interpretations of life by which people find meaning and to which they give commitment, and who would abolish school worship, are not necessarily opposed to the teaching of Christianity. I for one ask that Christianity may be interestingly, fully and positively taught and that its aesthetic, affective and cognitive aspects might be fully explored, so that the children leaving our schools may understand the contribution which Christianity has made to human life and know what it means to be a Christian in terms of practice, belief and commitment. If we can agree on this aim, perhaps the suspicions which exist among RE teachers can be replaced by co-operation in devising methods and materials which will enable it to be accomplished. Some of the best so far seem to have come from BBC Schools material, especially 'Radiovision' programmes, rather than the Church Missionary Society or commercial publishers.

PART THREE

This is an attempt to practise what I preach through encouraging three friends, who have made considerable contributions to the subject, to discuss religious education, or 'stances for living' as Harry Stopes-Roe would prefer, from their viewpoints. Please note the indefinite article in the title of their pieces. Just as there is no Christian consensus about RE, so there is much variety of attitude among Humanists, Muslims and Jews. In confining the opportunity of expression to members of these three groups, I have recognised that they are the most active and most critical non-Christians within the RE context at the present time. Each brings something distinctive which needs to be shared. The Humanist gives a naturalistic interpretation to human existence, and when he enters the RE debate he brings this with him. This should remind us that depth and quality as well as arriving at a coherent cosmology are not only of interest to religious believers. The Humanist presence requires us to avoid making over-claims for religion ('only religious believers care', 'only religious believers have a moral sense and a responsible approach to life'). Humanism in the classroom can not only require the religions to make honest statements, it is also potentially helpful to those many pupils who will not find the solution to their search for meaning in a religious outlook. The presence is also a reminder of reality; society is pluralistic, and RE needs to accept this openly.

The Jewish presence constantly reminds me of four things: the relationship between religion and family life, which must find its way into the syllabus; the need to recognise that the Old Testament is also the Jewish Bible, a complete scripture in its own right; the awareness that Judaism is a living faith, not something that came to an end at Masada; and the fact, which Christian students find almost impossible to grasp, that the Christian interpretation of messiahship differs considerably from that of Judaism. The impact of these must gradually percolate into the lecture-hall and classroom.

The Muslim asks me not to be so naïve as to think that a positive Christian RE syllabus will effect the spiritual revival that some people are seeking. His concern is for the total curriculum. If the values concealed within the study of literature, science or history are non-Islamic, religious studies as a subject cannot provide an antidote. I find Muslims clear-sighted in a way which only conservative evangelical Christians seem to be among other groups. The Muslim requires me as a parent and a teacher to consider what values education should be communicating.

Chapter 13

Religious Education:
a Humanist Insight

(1) Inspiration and Knowledge

The paradox of the activity known as 'religious education' is that it is concerned with knowledge of a kind that impinges most personally upon each individual—and yet there is no knowledge available. Religious education stimulates questions at the interface between fact and value, where we do not know the answers. Is my life meaningful? How can I find purpose in life? How can I find autonomy, and unite it with responsibility?

This is my starting-point: we do not *know*. But I must be careful here, for 'we do not know' can be taken in two ways: I might be saying that each of us *individually* does not know; or I might be saying that we *collectively* do not know. I mean the latter. The former may well be false. It may well be that there are many of us who, each in his own heart, knows that he knows. But there are contradictions between our different 'knowledges'. We cannot, therefore, add together each our different 'knowledge' and arrive at one collective 'knowledge'. One of us may 'know' that God exists; the next of us may 'know' that He does not; when we try to work together, we must both acknowledge that *we know* neither the one nor the other.

The situation I have pointed to is entirely impartial between all the possible different views. It is unfortunate that the word 'agnosticism' has come to be associated specifically with an attitude of doubt towards religious belief. It would be interesting to examine historically how this has come about, for the word means 'a-gnosis', 'without knowledge', and it really does no more than ask each of us for a touch of humility. To admit agnosticism is not to say that we are 'uncertain', nor to forgo the claims that we wish to make. No doubt *some* claims are in fact, at least roughly, true; the trouble is *we* do not know which!

The scope and significance of agnosticism depend on the range of the persons who are trying to work together, and what they are jointly trying to do. In this chapter I am concerned with county schools, and 'we' therefore extends over the range of views which characterises the Western liberal tradition as it is exemplified in Britain now. It is the essence of county schools that all children have equal access, and all should receive equal respect and concern. The activity we are engaged upon will, whether we intend it or not, affect the attitudes, values, sense of autonomy and so on of the children in our care; for in religious education we are touching upon the mainsprings of concern and motivation. (This is not to say, of course, that the results of what we do will be what we intend them to be!)

In this chapter I want to examine the implications for the RE curriculum, and for the way it is handled, of the two facts, first that the subject impinges in a particular way on the values, attitudes and concerns of pupils, and second that we collectively suffer from agnosticism concerning the foundations of values and so on. I do not mean that RE is unique in these respects, but it does raise these problems in a particularly sharp form. Conversely, the nature and the scope of RE have implications for its teaching beyond the curriculum. What degree of concern, involvement, personal commitment and so on should we expect of teachers? It seems to me that these qualities should be carried into the classroom. But each attitude requires a specific object. It is therefore important to see that the qualities required by agnosticism are openness of inquiry and fairness towards others, not a lack of personal conviction. We come together as Christians, Humanists and others to educate our children. If we are to do our job effectively, we must be whole persons, and manifest our wholeness. As whole persons we have convictions and we have uncertainties, as we have concerns and lethargies. The prime requirement of good education is that we should be honest with our children.

It seems to me that we must find a consensus if we are to operate county schools successfully. The foundation of consensus is fairness. But, because we are dealing with important matters, a mere negative fairness which says nothing is not good enough. I therefore propose the following principle to guide curricular considerations:

> *The principle of active fairness*: On matters within the scope of agnosticism, we must in education be fair to the range of views which are worthy of respect, while at the same time considering the evidence which bears on the matters in hand.

The qualification, 'which are worthy of respect', is necessary, or some alternative like 'which characterise the Western liberal tradition' which I used two paragraphs back, because otherwise everything is 'subject to agnosticism'! If one is to be realistic, one must strike a balance between the suppression of legitimate differences of opinion and the destruction of all worthwhile co-operative effort.

(2) *The Focus of Agnosticism*
I am concerned with agnosticism in a practical sense, not in a philo-

sophical one. It is relevant in certain areas, not in others. There is no real doubt about many trivial things—not about many very substantial ones. This is worth a moment's consideration. History, geography, languages, literatures, mathematics, sciences, all have a core of knowledge on which we do agree, and in a real sense this core is what matters most in each subject. Agnosticism only bears on these subjects in their more marginal areas, and in a subtle second-order sense implicit in the growth of knowledge. Even if we are all in agreement now, we must recognise that the future may hold surprises for us, and it is of the nature of the case that we cannot be *sure* where! A good teacher, therefore, will open the pupil's mind to the idea of growth, which implies that some of what he is learning may be wrong. But this is more procedural than practical. For the core areas of these subjects, the teacher can transmit to his pupils a sense of confidence and common agreement. The world *is* pretty much as the teacher says in these respects, even if the account may need *some* correction.

Agnosticism becomes paramount in two areas: politics and religion. The very framing of the questions one might ask is controversial. Some may talk of 'ultimate questions'; others reject the implications of such words. In what sense can one ask questions involving 'ultimate'? Classic 'ultimate questions' concern God, freedom and immortality. What are the presuppositions of one who asks such questions? Perhaps one reaches a common point of departure if one asks questions about the nature of man, of purpose and of duty. Of course, one can discuss these questions philosophically; but how can answers be framed, and how do they bear on the real purposes of real men and women? I have mentioned various kinds of questions one might set in the role of 'ultimate questions'. Must their answers, or the answer to any of them, be *central* to one's own sense of purpose in life? I ask these questions about questions for the purpose of pointing to the existence of controversy and difficulty, not to insinuate any particular answers.

It is by no means obvious what approach is fair to all views, and it will take a substantial co-operative effort to sort out such an approach. All I am attempting in this chapter is to disentangle a few threads.

There has been a habitual association of 'religion' and 'ultimacy' in all its various aspects—the very existence of meaning and purpose in life. There has also been a habitual association of 'religion' and 'God' (or other supernatural or transcendent order, state or power). Each of these associations separately could be merely a matter of the use of words; namely, each could turn on the way the word 'religion' is defined. The two associations together, however, necessarily carry the very substantial implication that 'God' is 'the real source of meaning

and purpose'. To put the point in practical terms, omitting possibilities of no importance: If it is necessary that all religions involve God,
and if anything that is an expression of the real source of meaning and
purpose counts as religion, then it follows that meaning and purpose
necessarily involve God.

I assume that 'God' has some significance, and is not merely an
empty label for whatever exists. Then the claim 'the real source of
meaning necessarily involves God' is a significant proposition. As
such it is not legitimate to formulate a definition which entails it. If
one wishes to say that religion necessarily involves God, then one must
allow that there are 'real' sources of meaning which are not religious.
Conversely, if one counts anything as a religion which is the
expression of the 'reality' of man's quest for meaning, then religion
does not necessarily involve God, and Humanism and Marxism are
religions. Either use is possible; they *cannot* be combined in the
definition of religion. One element or the other must go. Of course,
whichever identification is brought into the definition, a religious
person will want to maintain the other as a claim; this is quite proper,
but it is a substantial claim, and subject to agnosticism. It is not a
mere matter of the use of words.

Consensus seems to focus clearly on preserving the connection of
'religion' and 'God or other supernatural or transcendent order, state
or power'.* I will follow this use. We thus require a term to express
man's quest for meaning and purpose, *wherever and however he may
find it*. Some will find it in God; some will find it in his fellow-men
and the natural world. The term 'life-stance' or 'stance for living' is
coming to be used for this.** For a religious person, the centrality of
God, the Eternal, the Sacred, the Transcendent, is the supreme fact
about the Ultimate. Likewise the lack of reason for belief in any
transcendent or supernatural order, and hence the 'ultimacy' of the
natural world, is fundamental for the naturalist. Each is central to the
belief of each; but neither is part of the *definition* of 'life-stance'—so
this concept is shared by both.

It is no more possible to give a simple definition of 'life-stance' than
of 'religion'. Our purpose in forming the concept of a 'life-stance' is
to generalise the concept of a 'religion'. We are forming a wider
category of which religion is a species. Therefore, the impossibility of

*I will not continue to carry this qualification 'or other . . .'. The reader must under-
stand it. There are also technicalities about 'primitive' or 'tribal' religions, but I will not
go into these.
**'Life-stance', 'stance of life', 'stance of living', 'stance for living' are all variants of
the same term. I use them all, to keep the choice open. None of these versions is really
right, and I hope someone will come up with the perfect term. It is the concept, not the
term, that matters.

providing a simple definition of 'religion' is transmitted to 'life-stance'. The only fixed point of the latter is that a 'religious life-stance' is simply a 'religion'.

As the process of 'generalising' is difficult, I will give an analogy. Imagine that we are men in a society in which men and women are *entirely* separate—except for an Overlord who takes the food and other sacrifices of the men, and produces man-infants from the Temple. Then we know about men but not women; we would have no concept of 'human', as a wider concept distinct from 'man'. Now, suppose we begin to suspect the possibility of women. We will hardly be able to acknowledge it. We try to define a new generic concept 'human'. How would we do it? We have no clear simple definition of 'man', and even less can we expect a simple definition of 'human'. But if we can get the idea of 'masculinity' (corresponding to 'involving God (etc.)') we can think of 'human' as 'man' without specific masculinity. This would not make it any less the case that a male human being is fully male; and a female human being, equally, is fully female—and both are fully human. This is only possible, in fact, because 'human' implies neither masculinity nor femininity; it is impartial. Likewise, 'stance for living' implies neither God nor atheism, but a stance for living is either a religion or a non-religion. (We still lack a suitable word for a 'non-religion'. Likewise, the word 'fe-male' might be thought invidious, though its actual etymology is not what it looks to be.) Similarly, a 'male human being' is simply a 'man' (no more, no less), just as a 'religious life-stance' is simply a 'religion'.

Though one cannot give a real definition of 'life-stance', one can give an indication of its scope as a sort of quasi-definition:

A *life-stance* is whatever an individual finds to be involved in, whatever he finds as the ultimate source of meaning and purpose.

The recognition of this concept is fundamental for any adequate development of 'religious education', for the focus of agnosticism strikes just here: does the ultimate source of meaning and purpose involve God? *We* do not know.

(3) *Education for Meaning*

As I have introduced the concept of a stance for living, it is necessarily connected in a very intimate way with individuals' sense of meaning, purpose and commitment. These three concepts, and still others, are closely related, and I will not in this chapter attempt to resolve their relationships. More difficulty is introduced by the word 'ultimate' in the quasi-definition of life-stance. But first I want to establish the connections between 'life-stances', 'religious education' and 'meaning, purpose and commitment'.

Whatever the Source or sources of meaning and purpose may be, they clearly are at the heart of religious education. Even if the Theorist may restrict his expositions to the mere phenomena of practice and belief, he is not true to the significance of life-stances, as these are normally conceived by their exponents, if he does not acknowledge that these phenomena are considered important because they are appropriate (as the exponent sees it) to the most important aspects of reality. Whether one sees the world as governed by a vengeful God, as loved by a loving God, or as the locus of class struggle, in each case one believes that the vision penetrates to the heart of the matter.

The bearing of RE on meaning and purpose is generally acknowledged. To focus attention, I quote the following expression of its aim: to 'help the pupil to identify and answer for himself the fundamental questions on which a purposeful philosophy of life depends'. Similar statements are repeated over and over again: this comes from a DES publication of nearly ten years ago, which was expressing the then leading view. (*Reports on Education*, No. 58, 1969). A recent statement talks of 'enabling children to make intelligent and personal commitments'. (Association of Christian Teachers, *Religious Education: a Considered View*, March 1976).

It is clear that life-stances, as conceived in the previous section, are what the DES and ACT statements are pointing to. In circumstances where it can be assumed that the only possible source of purpose, or object of commitment, is God, then one may restrict one's attention to religious life-stances. On the other hand, in contexts where we cannot assume belief in God, or disbelief in God, the subject-matter must be religious and naturalistic stances of life together, and not specifically the religious ones. I look further at what this means below; the basic point is clear. What is not so clear is exactly how one should systematise the structures of understanding and commitment that people have.

I think one must distinguish various roles of a life-stance. First, of course, the observances prescribed may be considered to be expressions of one's duty to the Supreme Power. Again, the observances may be practised in part because they are looked upon as the source of Grace (for example) for the individual or community. Outside the range of specific observances, the life-stance may provide authority or legitimation for the rightness of actions. This is a very important function of a life-stance, and it is normal for a life-stance—such as Christianity—to be looked upon as providing in principle a full moral code of behaviour. Here, I think, we must begin to be careful.

The Christian theologian specialising in casuistry will be right to consider that his particular life-stance has important things to say throughout the moral sphere. My point is that this connection is rather abstract and theoretical: most people will consider the conclusion rather than the theoretical argument leading back to the central features of the stance. This is important, for though it may well be true that the life-stance is highly significant in practice for behaviour, and it may be true that this behaviour is an expression of the 'commitment' and 'purposes' characteristic of the stance, this is not to say that the stance is playing a part *in the mind of* the ordinary adherent. In other words, it may not be realistic to say of him that the stance to which he belongs is acting as a '*philosophy* of life' for him, nor that these adherences to moral values are expressions of a real 'personal commitment' to Ultimate Reality as conceived by the stance in question. Yet, in various senses and in various ways, a person's life-stance may play an important part in his purposes and commitments.

How much do ordinary people 'make intelligent and personal commitments', or have 'a purposeful *philosophy* of life'? These are wonderful ideals; but is the past failure of religious education due to a degree of self-deception in this area? Should we think more in much simpler terms? Should we think of 'proximate' rather than 'ultimate' questions, and the actual processes by which people find values?

I do not mean these sceptical remarks to suggest that religions are irrelevant, but only that, if one thinks of them in stylised terms, then RE is irrelevant. Religious life-stances should be conceived as encompassing practical purposes and commitments as well as the philosophies and high commitments that do (in some sense) 'stand behind' them. This move is reflected in current religious thought, in talk of 'folk religion', which is a topic that should be much further developed. The same point, though intensified, should be made with respect to naturalistic life-stances. The point is intensified, because the absence of a distinct Absolute for those who are not religious means that the formal 'philosophy' element in their life-stance tends to obtrude even less significantly.

In truth, is it not in the practicalities of ordinary life that *most* people 'make intelligent and personal commitments', and lead their 'purposeful life'? This is another 'role' of a life-stance. The philosophical background, be it supernaturalistic or naturalistic, is important, but we are more likely to present it in a way that is relevant to children—and adults—if we recognise it for what it is, a philosophical background. We may also be more ready and able to help children to realise a meaningful and purposeful life. Further, if children are not over-pressed, some may then find that Ultimate

Reality—be it their fellow-men, or God, or whatever—may come alive for them.

(4) *Objective, Fair and Balanced*

Stances of life may enter a child's education at various points, and in various ways. I have been concentrating on the central area of RE—namely, the child's own sense of personal commitment, and purposeful philosophy of life. The criteria of 'good education' here are not the same as in the other areas where life-stances may arise.

There are many ways in which there are, or could be, subtle interactions between parts of the curriculum and the beliefs implicit in different life-stances. More particularly, one might think that, as people of different faiths all share one world, therefore the child should have some understanding of the different ways in which other people structure their beliefs and attitudes, and find a dynamic in their lives. Again, as life-stances have in the past, and still do, influence the history and culture of the world, one might think that the child's education should take cognisance of this. I have written an essay on these matters, and the appropriate educational criteria, which I hope will be published elsewhere.

Special criteria apply where the teacher is operating in a way that may act upon the child's sense of purpose in life, and the way he personally is going to cope with being human—for here the teacher is subject to agnosticism. The basic requirements are honesty to what is known, and to what is not known. These requirements apply whether the teacher intends to act upon the child's susceptibilities or not, for the teacher cannot know what the effects of his actions may be.

The requirements of 'honesty' can be expanded, and I will use the three terms 'objective', 'fair' and 'balanced' to express three aspects. These words in normal use are not clearly differentiated, but I will define them as technical terms. 'Fairness' and 'balance' are evaluative concepts, and their implementation must be worked out co-operatively, with the benefit of the children in mind.

The three criteria 'objectivity', 'fairness' and 'balance' apply whenever the teacher is explicitly or implicitly impinging on beliefs concerning the answers to 'ultimate questions', not merely 'doing world faiths'. Thus, one can for example aid a naturalistic type of view by implying that questions are closed, without making anything explicit; or one can influence towards religion by implying the necessity of a 'transcendent'.

Objectivity requires that all that is said or implied on matters subject to agnosticism shall be detached from the authority of the school, and of the teacher acting as teacher. Objectivity refers to the form of what is said. One teaches *about* various life-stances, one does not *teach* any. There is no relevant doubt on what different groups of people believe. For example, Christians believe in the reality of God. Agnosticism applies to the reality of God itself. Thus the teacher can make assertions (if cautiously) about what Christians believe concerning God's existence; but he must not endow the claim 'God does not exist' with authority. It is to be recognised as no more than one position, or as a position held by certain people. The teacher may not allow 'God does not exist' to become detached from one or other of these qualifications, to be expressed as a self-contained statement which carries the implication of assertion.

It is important to note two things that 'objectivity' does *not* require:

First, it does not require that the arguments for and against the various positions on 'God's existence' shall not be put; I would argue, in fact, that such material should be included. Again, however, the premisses of these arguments, in so far as they are subject to agnosticism, must be presented 'objectively'. Simple categorical statements can only be made in respect of those premisses which are within consensus. Secondly, it does not require that the teacher shall pretend unconcern on God's existence; I would argue that the teacher should show his real concerns and commitments. 'Objectivity', as I use it, is not the same as 'detachment'; it requires, merely, that he *distinguish* between what can be said to be known and his own personal beliefs. There is no suggestion of 'It doesn't matter.'

It is difficult to describe positively what 'objectivity' requires. One might make the contrast: descriptive of beliefs about what is true/ assertive of what *is* true. If one is to do justice to the reality of beliefs, it is necessary to acknowledge that one is concerned with beliefs as to the truth; but to bring in 'beliefs' at all suggests a focus on 'belief' as against other aspects of a life-stance, and this is not entirely apt. The contrast is often put: phenomenological/confessional. But 'phenomenological' suggests an inadequate concern with beliefs, in favour of worship and other practices; and 'confessional' has very particular associations, which distort the contrast.

I think my opening definition of 'objectivity' puts the point best. But I will conclude with this more explicit, but rather simple, statement: the teacher explains what people believe about God, what people (believing about God) do as a consequence, and so on; he does not present the truth about God, or even the truth about God's existence. And he does not insinuate support or rejection, by the incidental use of phrases with evaluative overtones.

Fairness requires that the selection of material which bears on a particular stance for living shall not distort its status, either in respect of its verisimilitude or of its moral worth. Granted that the teacher will only assert positively such statements as are not subject to agnosticism, and which he may therefore reasonably present as 'true', he must make some selection from this potentially infinite range. 'Fairness' serves as a guiding principle. The demand for fairness must, of course, always be limited by the constraints of time, which are themselves determined by considerations of balance. It is easy to give a formal definition of this concept, but the definition introduces delicate value judgements which make it difficult to apply. There are no absolute standards to guide our selection of what to include and what to omit, nor our manner of presenting or of summarising facts. It is notorious that a 'fair comment' may seem fair to the person who makes it but unfair to the person who suffers it. By selection one can even suggest falsehood.

'Truth', 'objectivity' and 'fairness' are three distinct criteria. A false statement clapped in quotation marks and attributed to someone who actually made it becomes part of a whole which is both true and objective. But it may not be fair. One does not protect oneself simply by saying 'Fascists believed that Jews were destroying Germany.' If such a statement is made, it must be set in an adequate context. Again, it would be unfair to present Judaism as a sort of failed Christianity; such a presentation can be achieved without making a single false or non-objective statement.

In my opening definition of 'fairness' I included 'moral worth'. This raises difficult questions. What of the Inquisition? Or, in the contemporary world, what of the lack of civil liberties for 'non-believers' in certain Christian, Marxist and other countries? Does one present a solely favourable view of different stances? As a Humanist, I would wish that all stances, including Humanism, were presented as they are—fairly but with their faults.

Balance (as I use the term) refers to the relative weighting accorded to different points of view or, more particularly, different stances for living. The requirement of 'balance' implies that the weighting shall correctly reflect the importance of the view in question. 'Balance' is of fundamental importance because we are dealing with persons who are not fully mature. First, the importance that the pupils give to a particular view will tend to be moulded by the importance accorded to it in the teaching. Secondly, even adults are susceptible to repetition; even more so are children. Here one should notice that the requirement of 'objectivity' nominally protects the children from themselves asserting controversial beliefs—matters of substance which are subject to agnosticism, as they are presented by the teacher, are always prefixed or qualified in some way. But to rely on this alone is totally unrealistic. The qualification will not, in fact, be preserved in the pupil's mind, so repetition will become repetition of beliefs as if they were facts. Thirdly, a particular concentration on certain stances may (if it is well done, it should) stimulate interest in those stances. Finally, there are two further, related, points. First, pupils can not be assumed to be aware of possibilities unless the teacher tells them. Secondly, a pupil will only become significantly aware of a possibility if he is given time to absorb it slowly, and turn it over in his mind. I am expressing basic matters of importance; I am not here attempting to look at the serious problems that are implicit in each point. I must note, however, that it is helpful to take particular life-stances as examples, if it is made clear that this is what is being done.

The over-all importance of 'balance' has been well put by Colin Alves:

> If a school's curriculum does not include the study of religion then ... it might equally appear to be saying that religion is so irrelevant to normal living that the pupils need not bother to take account of it. (C. Alves in *New Movements in Religious Education*, ed. N. Smart and D. Horder (London: Temple Smith, 1975), p. 30.)

Colin Alves expresses this point with respect to religion, but a comparable point may be put with at least equal force with respect to naturalistic life-stances.

Fairness and balance are complementary concepts; and they share some features. They are complementary, for 'fairness' requires that all that is said on a particular stance for living shall be fair to *that* stance; 'balance' requires that all that is said on a particular point shall be fair to the *range* of stances.

'Fairness' and 'balance' share the feature of involving evaluations: the broad ideas are clear, but judgement is required in the borderline—which is where the real problems lie. One basic prerequisite for both concepts can be formulated objectively, however:

> No general restriction shall be applied to religious education which discriminates between one stance and another, from amongst those which are accepted as 'worthy of respect'.

Any decision as to how much attention shall be given to one stance or kind of stance, or how much support to one attitude or value, will of course depend on a particular assessment, according to criteria, of its 'importance'. This assessment will (no doubt) depend (in part) on the particular circumstances of the particular pupils. The point I am making now is that it is not legitimate to have a prior prejudice against any particular stance of living or kind of stance. A prime example of such prejudice is to conceive education in this area to be concerned with *religious* stances for living, with naturalistic stances introduced merely to illuminate the religious. This is what was required by the 1944 Education Act, as it was interpreted in Birmingham. (H. V. Stopes-Roe, *Learning for Living*, vol. 15, no. 4, Summer 1976).

Finally, 'fairness' and 'balance' are similar, in that both apply equally to those sections of a course which deal with specific stances, as well as those which deal with specific matters which are subject to agnosticism. The application to stance-specific material is obvious, but the other is equally important. Any discussion that bears on God or the after-life, for example, shall give a fair impression of the different views, and a balanced impression of their range.

These three concepts which I have indicated—objectivity, fairness and balance—together define the basic requirements of good education, where this is concerned with matters subject to agnosticism. These words do not, in natural use, have any clear-cut and distinct meanings. I have taken them over as the best words that I could find to express the concepts.

'Objectivity' covers the form and force of each statement made or implied by the teacher; he shall not give authority to one view as against another on matters in the range of agnosticism.

'Fairness' and 'balance' concern the content of statements made, and make specific reference to life-stances—

'Fairness' requires that those statements which bear on any particular stance for living shall together give a fair picture of its status, as to validity and value.

'Balance' requires that the statements which bear on any particular topic which is subject to agnosticism shall together give a picture of the views on the matter which is balanced over the range of stances for living. If one formulates 'the topic' in some broad and all-inclusive way, then 'balance' requires that the course as a whole (or, more generally, the education) shall help the pupil to appreciate the significance of different kinds of view on the nature of man and of purpose.

One may sum up all these requirements:

If the pupil moves on to faith, his journey must be without more support than would be given to a fellow pupil moving in an opposite direction. (D. G. Attfield, *Learning for Living*, vol. 13, no. 175, May 1974)

Here 'faith' must be taken to mean faith in any religious or naturalistic life-stance. If one makes a substantial statement on a matter of faith, if one is unfair for or against any stance, or if one dwells unduly on the views of any one stance or kind of stance, then one has given aid in the corresponding direction.

Those Humanists who like myself are now actively engaged in the development of religious education would bring the types of issues raised in this chapter to the debate.

Chapter 14

Religious Education: a Jewish Insight

Jews have always taken education seriously. According to rabbinic tradition, there were schools at the time of Abraham. Some scholars believe that, apart from the synagogue, the school is the most original institution created by post-biblical Judaism. The early rabbis taught that an ignorant Jew was a contradiction in terms, and that Jerusalem was destroyed because its children were in the streets and not in schools. So important was study that it was not to be interrupted even for the rebuilding of the Temple. It was permitted to turn a synagogue into a school, but not to turn a school into a synagogue. Torah scrolls were allowed to be sold in order to buy books for study. Thus, because the Jewish religion was a literature-sustained religion, it led to early efforts to provide elementary education for all the children in the community.

Teachers were held in high esteem. They and their students were considered society's most beautiful ornaments. An impatient man could not be a teacher, nor an unmarried one teach elementary classes. One was to revere a teacher as one reveres heaven. Some rabbis argued that teaching should be done gratuitously; others felt that teachers should not accept remuneration for teaching Torah, but might for teaching punctuation marks and accents! One union-minded rabbi declared that, if one sees cities uprooted, know that it came about because its citizens did not maintain teachers' salaries!

Parents were also called upon to educate their children. Pre-school education was vital and obligatory. A father was also expected to teach his children how to swim and train them for a future trade. Jewish education was therefore a product of the home, the parents, the community, and the teacher. Family and society determined the educational and spiritual progress of the future generation.

Jewish education was not confined to the Land of Israel. On the contrary, great centres of learning were founded in Babylon, and Jews experienced the Golden Age of learning in Spain prior to the expulsion in 1492. Later generations maintained their institutions throughout Eastern and Western Europe until Hitler destroyed most of them during the Second World War. The remnant has once again moved its tents of learning, in particular to the United States and Israel.

Modern Jewish education dates in the main from the end of the war. Jewish day schools have sprung up all over America, maintained by Orthodox and Conservative groups. In Britain there has been a steady growth of day schools in all cities and towns which have a sizeable Jewish community. Nevertheless, only about 17 per cent of Jewish children attend these schools. This means that just over 12,000 Jewish children, with a further 500 non-Jews, attend the fifty-five schools, ranging from kindergartens to high schools. Nineteen of these schools are state-aided. Most of them are run by various Orthodox groups, some by the Zionist Federation; but all adhere to Orthodox principles, and at present there are no schools run by the Reform or Liberal movements. Those in favour of denominational schools argue that Jewish education is of a higher standard; opponents feel that such schools segregate children and help to build a self-imposed ghetto. Obviously there are both advantages and disadvantages, and it would be premature to make any judgement at present.

Every Jewish day school devotes an amount of time for Jewish studies. This would include Hebrew language, both classical and modern Hebrew; Jewish history and religion. The time allocated varies from about one hour to four hours per day. As already mentioned, these lessons are conducted on Orthodox lines with little or no critical evaluation. To a similar extent this is the policy of Carmel College, the only Jewish public school in England.

The majority of Jewish children, therefore, attend state schools, and some Jewish parents share the same sentiments as adherents of other minor religions, no religions and even some Christians. Many make use of their right under the 1944 Education Act to withdraw their children from school assemblies and scripture lessons. This was very understandable when religious instruction meant religious indoctrination, and there is clear evidence that many a Jewish child suffered at the hands of an over-zealous teacher and was publicly informed that he or his people killed Jesus. Happily, this is now a rare occurrence, but it still rears its head from time to time. Where schools teach religious education or religious studies or even 'stances for living' there is less possibility of being sectarian and of teaching the superiority of Christianity. Many schools are now making a brave attempt to study world religions. Very few teachers have expertise in more than one non-Christian religion. The majority of schools lack the right resources. Too many depend on out-of-date text-books and audio-visual aids. Owing to recent cuts in education expenditure, with more to come, regrettably there will be fewer resources and courses for teachers, and just as changes and improvements were being made these cruel cuts will put RE back at least ten years, and it will still maintain its Cinderella status. In spite of this, many RE heads are making every effort in the teaching of world religions. It may be useful as well as necessary to enlist the help of experts; these in the main will be religious leaders in the community. Many rabbis, for example would be more than willing to address a class or group. In my opinion, this would be far better than a rabbi solely talking to a Jewish withdrawal class. In the main, these classes are counter-productive, and as long as religious education is being taught on modern lines they should be discontinued. Very often an unwilling Jewish teacher takes the class, or it is a free period or time for preparation for other subjects. Only rarely is it positive and, if it is, why exclude non-Jews? Let the whole class or year benefit. This, of course, holds true for all other minority religious groups.

A similar case can be made for school assemblies. In the past these have been acts of worship, and clearly non-Christians would feel that they could not participate. Hymns and prayers of a Christian nature would not be acceptable to members of other faiths. There would be less objection and more participation where assemblies are not specifically Christian, and if prayers are to be offered they should be readily acceptable to mixed groups. Again, a spokesman for one of the world religions could address the school. There are many Jewish festivals, for example, which could easily be mentioned in words and music during an assembly. It seems wrong and unfair that students begin the day with religious segregation. True religion should unite rather than separate.

On a personal note, my secondary school consisted of nearly 50 per cent Jewish boys, and all assemblies were totally acceptable. Hymns were general, and there was no mention of Jesus or Christian theology. At a later stage it was decided that on Mondays there would be separate Christian and Jewish assemblies. This proved a disaster from both points of view, and all agreed that it was a retrograde step. The majority Jewish view is clear: if the assembly is an extension of church worship, it should not include Jews. If it is inter-religious or non-religious, it must be for the whole school. I feel there is much scope for experimenting with assemblies, and would be reluctant to see them totally disappear. At the same time I find it intolerable to regard the assembly as a little church or synagogue service, with the head teacher acting the part of the minister and the students a reluctant congregation. An act of worship should not be confused with a spiritual experience to begin the school week or day.

Many RE teachers today are committed to the new approach. Some will obviously emphasise their own particular interest or expertise in one or more of the world religions, whilst others may wish to share the amount of time at their disposal with a general look at the beliefs and customs of mankind. From a Jewish point of view there can be a problem with the former method. Judaism, in some ways, is taken for granted since it is not an immigrant religion and has been part of the British scene for centuries. Jewish communities have flourished here for 300 years and, of course, up to the expulsion in 1290. There are some who view Judaism as a denomination within Christianity, and there is a danger that it is being ignored in favour of the more recent or Eastern religions now found in Britain.

Furthermore, there is an apparent lack of knowledge in many universities, colleges and schools with regard to the Jewish contribution in biblical and religious studies. How many teachers or students have heard of Claude Montefiore, for example, let alone read his many books? These include *The Synoptic Gospels* (1909), *Judaism and St Paul* (1914), *The Old Testament and After* (1923). This early leader of English Liberal Judaism is almost ignored, yet has made a worthwhile contribution. In our own time, Samuel Sandmell, Professor of Bible and Hellenistic Literature at the Hebrew Union College, Ohio, has made a significant contribution, acknowledged by leading theologians in America, but sadly hardly known in Britain. His publications include *The Hebrew Scriptures* (1963), *We Jews and Jesus* (1965), *The Genius of Paul* (1958), *A Jewish Understanding of the New Testament* (1956). Recently Oxford University Press has published Dr Sandmell's publications *Old Testament Issues* (1968) and *The Enjoyment of Scripture* (1972). Bible translators and commentators such as Harry Olinsky and Robert Gordis are also unknown names this side of the Atlantic. Hopefully tomorrow's students will not be deprived of their important publications.

A third problem in the teaching of Judaism is the lack of knowledge on the part of some teachers that Judaism is not solely based on the Old Testament. The new syllabuses of university boards for GCE are endeavouring to change this by requiring a knowledge of post-biblical Judaism including the Talmud, modern varieties of Judaism, etc. The problem is more apparent at primary-school level, and themes such as 'Jewish life in the time of Jesus' can give a false impression of present-day Judaism. It is also suggested that comparisons between temple and synagogue and priest and rabbi be emphasised and not regarded as extensions. It is also preferable to encourage students, especially younger children, to speak of rabbis and not vicars, and synagogues and not churches—not even Jewish churches!

It should be noted that many RE teachers make every effort to portray Judaism in the correct way, and the above comments must not be taken as a criticism against the whole profession. Improvements, however, can always be made.

We have so far considered the non-Jewish attitude to the teaching of Judaism. It is necessary to state the Jewish view on both the teaching of Judaism and the new approach to RE in general. There is, in fact, only *a* Jewish view, not *the* Jewish view; and, although these are personal observations, they are nevertheless shared by many Jewish educationalists and parents.

There is a minority feeling that, since Judaism is not a missionary religion, it is therefore only for Jews, so why should non-Jews be either interested or encouraged to learn about it? Such people would argue that Christians should worship and study their own religion, and Jews should do likewise, and never the two should meet. This *laissez-faire* attitude, it must be stressed, is a minority view not shared by the majority of Jews.

This group would be joined by another small group who would disapprove of Jews learning about Christianity—or any other world religion, for that matter. The New Testament would be forbidden territory. Some others would argue that it is a matter of priorities: limited time and the little knowledge Jewish children have about Judaism make it essential that other religions be neglected for the present. To a certain extent this is the policy of some Jewish day schools. Thus world religions plays little part in many of these schools, which many Jews may feel is wrong.

The overwhelming majority of Jews, however, welcome the opportunity to have a dialogue in religious education. The Board of Deputies of British Jews, representing all sections of Jewry, religious, political, social and charitable, has had for many years an Education Department and Speakers' Panel and has recently reformed its activities. The Education Department of the Jewish National Fund also gives information on both Judaism and Zionism and Israel. Two newcomers on the scene, the Jewish Information Service and the Jewish Education Bureau, offer publications, and speakers to schools, colleges and churches giving the views of both Orthodox and Progressive Judaism.

Schools and colleges through their RE periods have an important responsibility in presenting an accurate picture of Judaism. The broadcasting media have an even greater responsibility and on occasions have been guilty of misrepresentation. Programmes such as *Never Mind the Quality, Feel the Width*, and *My Son Reuben* may bring a few laughs, but they do an injustice. *Love Thy Neighbour* and *Till Death Us Do Part* are further examples of possibly increasing prejudice rather than diminishing it. The educational possibilities of television and radio are immense. Religious education can also benefit by improving the quality and perhaps even the quantity. There are possibilities that both the BBC and the various independent television and radio companies are prepared to play down the 'religious slot' on Sunday evenings between 6.15 and 7.30 for possible peak and early-morning or evening programmes during the rest of the week, with more time for non-Christian religions. Perhaps we will see *Songs of Praise* coming from a synagogue in the not too distant future. Non-Christian religious advisers should be sought in order to reflect present trends in world religions—which should not be left to other 'experts'.

An important aspect of modern RE is the desire to visit places of worship. An ever-increasing number of schoolchildren and college students now visit synagogues in all parts of the country. Some will come prepared; others will visit first, then study the religion. It is an advantage for younger children to be briefed prior to a visit. This can be done simply, and some of their questions can be written down in advance so that the most can be made of the visit. As it is normally the rabbi or minister who speaks to such groups, it is essential that time is not wasted. Most schools will make their visits during school-time. Some teachers may be prepared to devote a Friday evening or Saturday morning in order that the class may be present at a Sabbath service. A visit during the festivals of Tabernacles to see the Succah is also a possibility. Any visit is a concrete way of seeing another religion in operation and is far superior to even the best text-book. On a practical note it will be necessary to check up to see if any special dress is to be observed and whether the synagogue is Orthodox or Progressive.

A teacher can also bring a little of the synagogue or the Jewish home into the class, by bringing (or inviting a Jewish visitor to bring) a Menorah during Chanukah or items from the Seder table during Passover. It is, of course, far better to bring the real things rather than to rely on models or posters. The latter are better than nothing in cases where it is not possible to obtain genuine articles. One can and should encourage a Jewish member of class to bring an object from home and talk about its significance. It is essential, however, that one checks to ensure that the child is *au fait* with the subject as not every Jewish child or family has a knowledge or even an interest in Judaism.

It can therefore be clearly seen that most Jews welcome the current trends in religious education and are willing to make their contribution and co-operate with adherents of other world religions so that the understanding of different traditions and cultures can more easily be fostered and appreciated. In that way we can instil into our students a healthy respect for diversity and our pluralistic environment. We will then realise that uniformity is undesirable but unity is strength.

Chapter 15

Religious Education: a Muslim Insight

The first words of the revelation of God to the Prophet Muhammad in the Glorious Qur'an are:

Read! In the name of thy Lord and Cherisher, who created—created man, out of a (mere) clot of congealed blood: Read! And thy Lord is Most Bountiful,—he Who taught (the use of) the Pen,—taught man that which he knew not. (Qur'an, 96: 1-5.)

This verse shows us clearly that God is the source and only source of all knowledge in which man can find the secrets of life and the universe.

Islamic education, therefore, does not mean religious education by itself at the expense of art and science. In fact, Islam is the religion in which there is no place for what is known as 'religious' or 'secular' areas of life. It takes life as one unit and does not admit tight compartments in it, one out-weighing the other. Fundamentally, it is an attitude and a way of life having certain ideals and ethical values, with a practical system covering the whole range of human activity, based upon a belief in the oneness of God and in the Day of Judgement when man stands in front of God. It lays down definite principles of morality and law which govern all social affairs as well as individual conduct and state affairs. It is thus a system of belief with moral and legal aspects which encompass the entire field of human life. Every action must be for God and the seeking of God's pleasure. Thus, the whole life of a Muslim is worship (Ibadah).

Education in general, and religious education of the young in particular, is the main duty of the parents. The Prophet Muhammad (peace and blessing of God be upon him) said:

When a person dies, his actions come to an end except in respect of three matters that he leaves behind, a continuing charity, knowledge from which benefit could be derived and a righteous child who prays for the parent.

The Prophet also said:

The learned ones are the heirs of the Prophets, they leave know-

ledge as their inheritance; he who inherits it, inherits a great
fortune.

Also:

> Seeking knowledge is obligatory upon every Muslim man and
> woman.

Education in Islam is the learning of how one should live and develop
throughout one's own life. It is aimed at formulating individual self-
consciousness within membership of the community. Therefore, the
whole concept of education is based on religious education as the
foundation of moral conduct and practical living; that is why learning
is placed on an equal footing with worship in Islam.

Since the advent of Islam, the mosque has been the centre of all
activities. It was the place from which the Prophet, and the Caliphs
after him, managed affairs of state; it also served as the centre for the
education of the Muslim community. It developed at the time of the
rise of Islam, and less than a century after the Prophet became the
foundation of the school system which ever since has functioned on a
voluntary basis. These mosque schools (Kutab or Maktab) serve now
for pre-school education. The oldest such school—Al Azhar in
Cairo—however, developed into a university not only for religious
education, but also for secular subjects such as engineering and
medicine. It teaches all subjects, as it did during the first century of
Islam, when the entire society was motivated by the Qur'anic
revelation and the teachings of the Prophet. Instruction and
discussion were the prime methods of education for the learned
Muslims at the mosque. These were conducted on an individual basis
or in groups circled around the teacher, all sitting on the mosque floor.

The whole aim of education is to open the minds of men to look at
the universe and discover what might be of good service to mankind as
vice-regent of God on this earth, opening hearts and strengthening
faith in the creator of all things. The Qur'an reflects this clearly in:

> Do they (mankind) not look at the sky above them? We have made
> it and adorned it. And the earth, We have spread it out and set
> thereon mountains standing firm, and produced therein every kind
> of beautiful growth (in pairs), to be observed and commemorated
> by every devotee turning (to God). (Qur'an, 50: 6-8.)

Also:

> Behold! In the creation of the heavens and the earth, and the

alternation of Night and Day, there are indeed Signs for men of understanding. (Qur'an, 3: 190.)

It is as products of this basic teaching that we see the great men and women of Islam such as Ibn Arabi, Avicenna, Al-Biruni, Ibn Rashd and Al-Ghazzali. They were not only specialists in their own subjects, but also scholars in other fields, particularly education and philosophy.

Although the mosque is the institution and centre for learning, the home is the place of inspiration where a secure foundation for living is laid. The mother is the source of such inspiration and the maker of men. In this connection the Prophet said: 'Heaven is under the feet of mothers.' The education of the female partner of man is based on an equal footing according to the teachings of the Qur'an. This was observed in early Islam, but unfortunately changes have taken place during the last few centuries owing to many factors—political and social—and illiteracy among the whole nation.

The intelligentsia of the Muslim community today especially those who have been educated or are living in the Western world, attach great importance to the education of their daughters. To balance this education, which is often secular, great attention is also paid to religious education at home and in the mosque.

Although old-fashioned methods are followed in teaching children at the mosque, the system is effective and produces a generation aware of its duty to God and society.

Muslims, in spite of the many political changes in their countries, are far more aware of religious education than any other religious society in the rest of the world.

The home is the place for inspiration, the school has the duty to strengthen this. Thus the functions of the school should be:

(1) To translate religious belief into a practical aspect of life. For example, when talking about Zakat, the purification of wealth, and the five daily Prayers as the purification of soul and body, we also look at the whole economic and social system, as well as the requirement to do good to the poor and needy as an obligation upon the individual.

(2) To mould religious morals into the behaviour of the individuals. If we say God is merciful and kind, we have to be merciful and kind to others as God loves those who follow his way.

(3) To pave the way for free discussion without commitment. Teachers or persons in charge should simply state the facts and examine them without any personal judgement.

(4) To leave the choice to the pupil without direct or indirect

influence from the teachers with due respect and consideration for the parents' wishes.

Therefore, the aim of the school should be not to indoctrinate the pupil, but to give him the insight to search and find out for himself. This might seem to be wishful thinking; unfortunately the secularisation of the school system today contradicts this aim as faith in God is not the guardian of research in all fields. It is hoped that teachers of religious education will be believers in God, guardians and upholders of the spirit and faith of those in their care.

The aim of religious education in Islam is to establish:

(1) Self-conscious belief in one God as the Creator and man as his vice-regent on earth.
(2) Faith and hope in the Creator.
(3) The revelation of God as the source for moral conduct in respect of all aspects of life.
(4) Through the belief in God:
    (*a*) the love for the truth should grow and seeking the truth become a duty for every Muslim;
    (*b*) the love of doing good and preventing evil should thrive;
    (*c*) all actions should be for the sake of God.

There is a widespread view that Britain is no longer a Christian country. On the face of it this might be true. The devout Christian is in the minority, but the heritage of Britain is Christian, and this helps the Christian believer to the extent that, although in a minority, he is not looked on as a stranger. Other religious minorities, especially in areas where there are not many immigrants, look very strange to the host community. Thus, the Muslim sometimes finds it very difficult to explain his behaviour according to his belief.

Parents and religious authorities in every community, including the Christian, agree that, owing to the change in society, the moral standards in schools today are much lower than, let us say, twenty years ago. Therefore, the Muslim community feels that, whatever inspiration the Muslim home gives the child, the atmosphere at the school and other establishments will contradict it. The reason is that moral values today have a different aim. In the past we tried to do good and help others without looking for a reward except from God. Today we are selfish and always on the lookout for material gain. Christianity today has also relaxed its moral attitude towards sex, the relationship between male and female is more free, while Muslims still carry on believing that prevention is better than cure and will continue to do so.

This leads us to some problems facing Muslim youth at school in

Britain. One of the anxieties Muslims have about co-education is that education should develop the role of the individual in the society, and thus the education of girls should be in line with their future role as mothers. The co-education of boys and girls will not cater for this.

There are many fundamental problems which Muslims face when sending their children to school in Britain, such as the uniform, food, leave for Muslim holidays, and physical education. Most of these problems could easily be solved if Muslim parents were made aware of their rights under the 1944 Education Act. A close contact between the parents and the school or education authority helps greatly in overcoming these difficulties. Unfortunately, the Muslim parent, perhaps owing to language difficulty, semi-literacy or social circumstances finds it difficult to maintain close contact with schools. It has been noted that Muslim parents very rarely participate in school functions such as 'open evenings', 'parent-teacher associations', 'sports days' and other events.

The Muslim community in the West has not yet passed the period of struggle to correct the image of Islam created hundreds of years ago by the Crusaders and Orientalists. We are at the stage of acquiring recognition. This is shown very clearly in the new trend of religious education today in schools to include Islam in the syllabus. This is due to the change within a society which became multi-racial and multi-religious.

From experience, there appears to be a great struggle between the educationalists who like to expose the child to many fundamentals in a factual way, which at times are even contradictory, and the religious authorities who see richness and true worth in all faiths. We feel that there is a great deal to be learned from each other, and each community can contribute to the integrity of man and respect for the individual. Muslims believe that material progress cannot fulfil its purpose unless it is accompanied by a change of morals and character. Selfishness, lack of honesty and the neglect of duty to one another are the roots of destruction. A moral revolution in our educational system is sadly lacking; we Muslims could contribute to bringing it nearer by sharing in a straightforward confrontation of all faiths with the materialistic world. The religious education teacher should not only be armed with the correct and sound knowledge of other faiths, but he should also be given the moral resources and the spiritual values which they contain. We believe that Islam is rich in such resources which the teacher and the authors of books for RE could bring to the notice of students.

The five Pillars of Islam, for example, could be taught in a more interesting way by looking at their inner meaning rather than by looking only at the physical aspects. We read in the Qur'an:

Say You (Muhammad): We believe in God and in that which has been sent on us and sent down on Abraham, Ishmael, Isaac and Jacob and the tribes, and that which was given to Moses and Jesus and the Prophets of their Lord. We make no division between any of them and to Him we surrender. (Qur'an, 2: 136.)

The prime duty of the Muslim is to accept and believe in the prophets of God who came before the Prophet Muhammad (peace and blessing of God be upon them all), this gives the insight that we could learn from each other and contribute to a respect and recognition for each other. And when the Qur'an states, 'O mankind: We have created you male and female, and have made you nations and tribes that you may know one another. Lo, the noblest of you in the sight of God is he with the best conduct. Lo, God is all-knowing, aware' (99: 14), we see that Islam recognises the differences and accepts that there cannot be compulsion in religion and the noblest of all is the one with the best conduct. That is our aim in religious education and that is our hope.

To fulfil this aim we believe that the various religious communities should be encouraged to draw up an outline of the relevant material for teaching at different levels and to suggest and give examples of such material to be used in the schools. Students of different religious backgrounds should be encouraged by their teachers to take an active part in religious education lessons by asking them to present projects about their own religion or to lead a discussion or organise an assembly with the help of the teacher.

A half-hearted attempt (which is often termed 'neutral') to present religious studies will not solve man's problems, especially when one considers the present permissive age where alcohol, drugs, unwanted children, unmarried mothers and associated anti-social or degraded standards create serious social problems.

It is felt that a complete overhaul of all religious studies should be undertaken, since present plans often give rise to a lack of optimism for the solving of the problems of our own Muslim community in Britain.

As a last resort, it is felt that the right to withdraw one's children from RE should be the prerogative of all parents, but only on the undertaking by the parents of a promise to provide from home or through the community of his own choice the necessary religious education within his own faith, for the responsibility is heavy.

The Islamic view of all education, including religious education, is dominated by the belief: we are all created by God, and to him we return.

Chapter 16

Removing the Illogicalities

Religious education is a subject which is very much alive and in good health. There have always been Christians ready to criticise it and struggle with its difficulties, and eager to improve the teaching of the subject, and now Humanists, Jews and others are joining them, bringing their own insights and challenges. It is amazing what strokes have been played by people with one foot chained to the crease by an Act of Parliament which was, at least to some extent, intended to dictate their stance. Teachers like myself, Christian, may not find the strictures very severe; being right we can move our front foot with comparative freedom, but the left-hander who is required to adopt our stance finds himself defeated! If Christians really wish to open up the subject to members of all faiths, they must remove a number of illogicalities!

Most obviously there is the statutory requirement to hold an act of worship. Christians may argue over the intentions of the Act, and the definition of the word 'worship', but they must not expect Jews and Muslims to take part in such acts of theological gymnastics; neither must they, when they have completed them to their own satisfaction, expect to have impressed Humanists. As for pupils, the whole exercise is often beyond them. If the act of worship is to remain—and a number of Christian specialists in religious education have recently suggested that it should not—it must be separated from the classroom subject of religious studies. It is impossible to be open-minded in the classroom and God-affirming (a major element in all worship save, perhaps, Theravada Buddhism) in the hall, and it is wrong to expect specialist teachers to provide worship-material or conduct acts of worship. In the kind of future which I envisage there may not be a Christian religious studies specialist in the school. Would it be right for a Jew to produce a Christian act of worship, or should the Jew ask pupils to join him in his worship? The question requires an answer. In some schools today a lone Christian is attempting to produce a Christian act of worship knowing that no member of staff and few pupils go to church and can really be called Christians. His position seems little different from that of a Muslim attempting to put his act of worship before the whole school and invite participation. The difference lies, of course, in the residual cultural legacy of Britain, which is Christian, not Muslim.

Were the Act to be repealed tomorrow the illogicalities would not disappear. People would still abuse the subject in one way or another. Some would ask too much of it—like a headmaster I worked with, who regarded me as the one who gave moral and spiritual tone to the school regardless of what he and the rest of the staff stood for. When society as a whole was Christianity-supporting it was possible to believe that RE transmitted the spiritual and moral heritage of the community. Now we see that one man cannot act effectively without the assent, backing and goodwill of the community. Assent for being an evangelist the RE teacher no longer has.

This does not mean that I have no responsibility for insights, behaviour and the general well-being of children; but, to be realistic, I have no more than my colleagues, than parents or the community at large. More must not be expected of me, and I must not make outrageous claims. Sadly, RE may be the only caring subject, the only opportunity which a pupil has to consider the meaning of life; but it need not be, it should not be, and we must be careful of trying to keep it on the timetable by saying that it is. Specialists in RE have, almost universally, rejected the role of evangelist, but an ambivalence still remains. Many still claim that the subject is unique and somehow wish to hang on to some position of privilege. Each subject is unique. Granted this, what added ingredient does religious studies possess? I cannot argue that it alone is concerned with understanding, explaining and interpreting existence. Scientists, artists and historians could also claim to share this interest. Each discipline has, however, a distinctive way of going about the task and a particular contribution to make, and it may be better to settle for the word 'distinctive' rather than to make assertions of uniqueness. Religious studies is concerned with beliefs and ritual practices in a way which other disciplines are not. The historian or student of literature may be interested in the Bible, and the anthropologist may find the religious practices of a Hindu village fascinating, but not in the same way as a person would whose interest is the religion of the Bible or Hinduism. A philosopher may discuss the possibilities of miracles occurring, the scientist may discount them as contrary to his knowledge of natural laws, but the theologian, whether he accepts them or not, has still to understand what the writers of the gospels or the janam sakhis were asserting about Jesus or Guru Nanak when they included miracle stories in their narratives. Religious studies, then, has special interests which are its peculiar concerns. It should make sure that school RE remains faithful to these aims and neither exceeds them nor abdicates its responsibilities by, for example, reducing the subject to community service. How the great traditions assert the relationship of man to the cosmos, and how they express this relationship, is the first task of religious studies—put more simply, what it means to be a Christian or a Muslim or a Humanist in terms of belief and practices. Let the historian, the human-geography specialist and the sociologist combine to study the settlement of Jews in Leeds—but then I must say that the task is not yet complete. It remains for me to explain the beliefs and practices of a living community.

The inclusion of world religions may be leading us back from an almost total concentration on the social gospel. The pendulum could, of course, swing too far in the opposite direction, so that RE became so discipline-orientated that it ceased to care for the well-being of the children it taught. The remedy, I suggest, lies not in the content but in the person. I have suffered under a PE teacher so concerned about the health of the body that the fearful humanity inside it shivered in unnoticed misery. We all know of teachers for whom the subject alone exists, especially in secondary schools, and have met some RE teachers who fall into this category if we are honest, as well as knowing warm-hearted teachers of mathematics or technical drawing—to name subjects in which a precise clinical approach might be expected to the detriment of human relations.

We must not forget that part of religion has to do with relation-ships. 'Love your neighbour' is the ethical teaching about which most faiths agree. Even if moral education should emerge as a subject separate from RE it could never be ignored by it. However, to mention another illogicality, it is surely wrong for Christians to claim that 'love your neighbour' is a teaching peculiar to them. The words were spoken by a Jew to Jesus (Luke, 10: 27), quoting from the Torah (Leviticus, 19: 18), yet RE courses on social and moral responsibility are usually concerned with 'the Christian...', or more honestly 'a Christian attitude to...', and not with conveying the truth that Humanists or Parsees are also responsible people with sophisticated codes of ethics. No one who has met Jews or Humanists, or who has read sufficient to teach about their beliefs, can honestly perpetuate the prejudice that 'only Christians care'.

Concepts as well as practices and beliefs are the concern of those systems which are classified generally as religions and of those who study them. What is meant by the word 'God', what questions are posed by the assertion that miracles do or do not happen, how suffering is to be understood and explained—these are issues which later rather than sooner the pupil needs to be helped to consider. The teaching techniques have yet to be worked out. Often implicit in those who accept Goldman's findings is the assumption that the ability to form concepts or handle abstract ideas will take place naturally. Anyone who has taught mature students or joined a church discussion group should know better. Growth seems to stop at thirteen plus, even if the student takes 'O' levels or even 'A' levels. This is not something peculiar to religious studies; it is true also of history. A student may have a sound knowledge of a period but lack the ability to enter it. His study of the Romans or the Tudors is from a twentieth-century standpoint. So long as the emphasis is upon memorising and regurgitating information the need to understand concepts will not exist and teachers will not do anything about it. The solution to the problem lies in confronting pupils and students with concepts in a type of education which transcends the descriptive. This can be done through the medium of Christian studies, Humanism, Hinduism or philosophy; but even the latter, as many of us know well, need be no more than memorising the arguments for and against the existence of God. If RE teachers argue that theirs is the 'only thinking subject', they are wrong; most subjects can challenge the pupil to think seriously and conceptually—and often RE does not.

A new confessionalism has also arisen as a by-product of the world religions movement. An eagerness to convert pupils to the acceptance of a religious view of life has sometimes replaced the desire to induct them into the Christian faith. Consequently, there are those who would accept that it is proper to teach children about Islam but would not wish to include religion—challenging interpretations of life, such as Humanism and Marxism. However, if we wish to enable the pupil to understand the major belief systems which dominate the minds of mankind today, we can scarcely avoid studying the most powerful influence of all—Marxism. If we claim a distinctiveness for our discipline, we cannot leave it to the historian, for ideas are not his prime concern, or to the current affairs session unless somehow we are involved in it. But how is Marxism to be studied, fairly, on its own terms (as we study Islam) or critically from the point of view of Christian (or religious) apologetics? The half-way house of studying Marxism or Humanism to 'highlight the distinctive features of religious faith' (Birmingham Agreed Syllabus 1975, p. 10) cannot be tolerated for long.

It might be asked at this point what future there is for the Agreed Syllabus itself. 'None' might be the instant reply. Certainly, there would be no need for agreement between the Christian denominations; that situation is already a thing of the past. Indeed, the Birmingham syllabus controversy of 1974 seems to have been more political than religious, and certainly the Christian members of the Syllabus Conference and the Christian denominations of the United Kingdom as a whole did not oppose the inclusion of Marxism. In other words, RE is being left to the specialists in schools, colleges and universities. It is being taken out of the religious arena. I hope that the Muslim presence will not revive the confessional interest. Muslim help is needed to provide specialist knowledge on Islam, and to share as educationalists in the work of RE, but not in invoking the Act and restricting curriculum development. Agreed syllabuses in the old sense belong to the past, as the Birmingham Syllabus shows, but handbooks like Birmingham's *Living Together* (1975) can encourage accurate, sound teaching and perhaps prevent children being taught the parable of the Good Samaritan five times. My daughters would have benefited if similar handbooks on history or geography had been on their teachers' shelves. So, let the syllabus die. Long live handbooks! There will always be a need for specialist bodies like the Christian Education Movement primary panel or the Shap Working Party to undertake precise tasks, beyond the skill of most local education authorities. Department of Education and Science money might be directed to such groups to enable them to organise working parties for specific purposes.

The implications for colleges of education of the approach to RE outlined in this book are probably less than for university theology departments. Once these taught prospective clergymen only. Now they do not. Some of their students may have no religious beliefs and know more about worship in a synagogue than in a church. If they are giving a theological education to future RE specialists, perhaps they should consider what form such training should take—even laying aside vocational considerations it might be salutary for them to compare their syllabuses with those of twenty years ago. Sometimes the updating process seems to have been one merely of adding a textual study of Buddhism or Islam, Pannenburg and a few other modern theologians. The pluralism and multi-faith nature of the community which lives within ten miles of the university is only slowly making an impact upon course content and academic attitudes. Far more serious is the fact that some universities which teach religious studies and theology make no provision for RE method to be acquired in their departments of education. The impression conveyed is that religious studies is not a worthwhile teaching subject. The message is given not only to theology graduates but also to their peers in history or science. We must remember that these are the college lecturers, headmasters, advisers, HMIs and chief education officers of the future. A strategy for the training of RE teachers should begin with the universities, not with colleges of education.

Finally, we must place world religions in education within its complete school and society context. If it now takes life as its base, and ranges widely and deeply as it explores the ways in which mankind attempts to make sense of life, it is in a position to encourage history, literature, to be less ethnocentric and to invite science to join in the search for a cosmology. Freed from the inhibitions of the past it becomes a subject which has an important part to play in framing a curriculum for the future. The nature of the world of the year 2000 I cannot envisage, but I do know that 1945 is far behind us and ever receding, though we still seem to be preparing our pupils to live in it, and I also know that children entering schools in 1980 will scarcely have completed their higher education when the new century dawns. However jaundiced I may feel on a Monday morning or a Friday afternoon, I try to keep that fact in my mind so that I may struggle to contribute to a curriculum which will match it.

The real revolution in religious education is only beginning. The 1944 Act still keeps us anchored to a religious stance rather than open inquiry into how man interprets his existence; school worship still suggests that openness is a sham and induction, not study, is the real purpose of school religion. A Muslim imam can still apply to a college to take religious studies and be guided into chemistry because he might find it difficult to obtain a specialist RE post, and a syllabus which includes Humanism and Marxism is still a syllabus of religious instruction. However, I am convinced that, though the Act needs to be changed and the name of the subject is inadequate, the future lies neither in law nor title but in serious debate and in an education system managed by people who from university to infant school are concerned for the subject and for the child. I am equally convinced that we should not necessarily be seeking for some sort of consensus. This is a popular word at the moment but, as this final chapter has perhaps shown, many issues exist for consideration, and agreement is unlikely. The teacher of RE, just like the child growing up in the late-twentieth-century world, must expect a journey but no map, for he is entering a new world, and he will have to work out his own route for some time yet. I hope this book will have shown that to travel hopefully is possible and have suggested that we can find our bearings. My concept of a destination emerges now and again on the pages, but I hope this will be seen as optimism and my own personal need for a goal, not as arrogance.

Appendix

Teaching World Religions in England and Wales

*This paper was originally published in German in *Thema Weltreligionen*, U. Tworuschka and D. Zillessen (eds.) published by Diesterweg (Frankfurt) and Kosel (Munich) 1977.

Less than ten years ago the place of world religions in education was marginal. At the time of writing the situation has dramatically changed to such an extent that a 'world religions approach' to religious education has apparently become accepted as normative.

This change can most easily be illustrated by reference to two 'Agreed Syllabuses drawn up by Local Education Authorities as guidelines for all those responsible for religious education in the schools of their areas'.* The first is that of the West Riding of Yorkshire, produced in 1966.** It can be summarised as follows:

Early Childhood: 4-7 Years
Introduction to God's care through an exploration of the natural environment and relationships; biblical associations to arise from living experiences connected with the following themes: Homes and Families; Autumn and Harvest; Winter and Christmas; Spring and Easter; Summer and Whitsun; Friends and Followers of Jesus.

Middle and Late Childhood, Pre-Adolescence: 7-11 Years
Religion is the essence of all life, illustrated by material from everyday experience, the Bible and other sources in such themes as: Caring, Thankfulness, Courage, Forgiveness; Sheep and Shepherds, Wells and Water, Corn and Bread, Highways and Journeys; Discovering the Bible; Life in Bible Times; and Christian Festivals.

Early Adolescence: 11-13 Years
Discovering Jesus: highlights in Jesus' life based on Mark's gospel.

*Agreed syllabuses have served a dual purpose. They have defined a common basis for religious education in a society which disagrees over questions of religious truth. Yesterday the disagreement was primarily between different Christian denominations, today between religions and over non-religious stances for living. They have also provided help for teachers seeking to teach the subject without any specialist knowledge. They have existed since the 1920s, but were required of all local education authorities by the 1944 Education Act. Cf. J. M. Hull 'Agreed Syllabuses, Past, Present and Future' in N. Smart and D. Horder (eds), *New Movements in Religious Education* (London, Temple Smith, 1975), pp. 97-119.

**County Council of West Riding of Yorkshire Education Department, *West Riding Agreed Syllabus: Suggestions for Religious Education* (Wakefield, 1966).

Discovering Christianity today: the New Testament Church; Church History; the Church in the twentieth century.

Middle Adolescence: 13-16 Years

Christian worship and practice: in Old and New Testaments and today.

Personal relationships: Love and Responsibility with reference to the New Testament and contemporary problems.

Christianity in the modern world: questions about the Bible, Jesus, God, Sin, Suffering, Prayer, the Church, Science and Religion.

World Problems: media; hunger; work and leisure; gambling; refugees; illiteracy; world religions.

Late Adolescence: 16-18 Years

Religion and life in contemporary society: religious faith; unity of the Bible; Christian doctrine; Christian morality; Alternatives to Christianity; Comparative Study of Religions; Christian Deviations; Christianity and the Arts; Science and Religion; the Ecumenical Movement; the Liturgical Movement.

The influence of this syllabus was not confined to the north-east of England, and similar emphases are to be found in subsequent syllabuses produced in Hampshire, Kent, Lancashire, London and Wiltshire. Its most noticeable characteristic is an attempt to relate the biblical concerns that had predominated in previous syllabuses to the present world of pupils. In this, the contemporary Christian theological concern with 'finding God in the midst of life' had conspired with warnings of developmental psychologists about 'unreadiness' for handling religious concepts in junior years.* As in all previous syllabuses, however, world religions is confined to a minor role even in late adolescence.

The second syllabus has recently emerged from the city of Birmingham.** Its contents can be summarised as follows:

Infancy and Early Childhood: 3-8 Years

A selection from each of the following topics: Festivals—Christian, Hindu, Jewish, Muslim and Sikh; Rituals and Customs—in family

---

*For the shift from Bible to Life themes, cf. 'Varieties of Religious Education', in *Religion*, vol. III, no. 1, Spring 1973, pp. 52-65. The preface to the West Riding Syllabus singles out Dr R. J. Goldman for special thanks during the preparatory stages.

**City of Birmingham Education Committee, *Agreed Syllabus of Religious Instruction* (Birmingham, 1975). This is unusually short. It consists of four pages of introduction and a four-page syllabus. The accompanying handbook is less prescriptive, but much more substantial in size; it contains suggestions to assist teachers drawing up new schemes of work. *Living Together: a Teacher's Handbook of Suggestions for Religious Education* (Birmingham, 1975).

and religious community; Stories from World Religions; Wonder and Mystery in the Natural World; Relationships with Others—illustrated by examples from world religions.

Later Childhood: 8-12 Years
Religious ideals and aspirations expressed in family and community life.
   Religious faith as represented by festivals and customs.
   Religious faith as represented by sacred places and the observances associated with them.
   Sacred writings preserving and inspiring traditions of religious faith; their distinctive language and literary form.
   Ways of living illustrated by stories of founders and great exemplars of world faiths and humanism.

Adolescence: 12-16 Years
Direct study of religion: Christianity and choice of up to three other religious traditions, including a non-religious stance for living.
   Indirect study of religion: religious beliefs, values and attitudes as relating to select topics in personal and social ethics.

Sixth Form
Further study of Adolescent topics.
Study in depth of such topics as: Buddhism; philosophy of religion; religion and arts; mysticism; etc.
   This and the accompanying handbook represent five years of collaboration between teachers from schools, colleges and universities, with representatives of all the local religious communities. The thoroughgoing concern with all manner of religious and non-religious life-stances, as well as Christianity, is evident even in the approach to the infant classroom. Initial anxieties on the part of certain local politicians about the inclusion of Communism, even as the negation of religion, did delay the publication by some months, and the controversy persists. But the syllabus now carries official status in accord with the 1944 Education Act. If the importance of world religions in the curriculum has been given this degree of public recognition, no one familiar with the pressures of institutional inertia within local government and educational administration can deny that a revolution has occurred.

IGNORANCE UNCHANGED AND UNCHALLENGED

However compelling these signs of revolution, their impact is as yet limited. Extensive ignorance persists in the community at large about the variety of religious belongings to be found in England and the world. Even the simplest features of different religious identities are apparently beyond the ken of many pupils and their parents.* Instead, prejudice-ridden images of a few religious allegiances are still rife. Among Christians, Catholics may be described as 'worshipping Mary', Protestants as 'not believing very much', and Jews as 'mean'. Jews and Muslims may speak bluntly of Hindus as idolaters; or Sikhs tell tales of Muslim murderings. To a Humanist, religious belief may mean 'anti-intellectual oppression'; in turn, he may be regarded by the religious believer as an 'agent of Lucifer'. The negative attitudes implicit in such views can easily interfere with attempts to provide more sympathetic perspectives.

Even if all teachers were free from any such distortions, they might yet define their own position about religious education—positive, negative or indifferent—in terms of the presuppositions of the older Agreed Syllabuses. Indeed, the persistence of the legal requirement for a daily act of worship,** invariably understood as Christian, in all schools may encourage them to do so. The pressures involved are illustrated by the following statistic on the personal beliefs of staff, given in a recent report on religious education in primary schools.*** Of teachers in selected schools, 1.9 per cent described themselves as atheists, 7.2 per cent as agnostics, 16.7 per cent as Humanists, 31.1 per cent as nominal Christians, and 43.1 per cent as committed Christians; of headteachers in the same schools, 3 described themselves as non-committed Christians, 47 as convinced. The leap in the extent of conviction can be variously interpreted, but it is difficult to avoid reading it as other than evidence of continuing institutional bias towards Christianity.

On the other hand, however willing individual teachers and head-teachers might be to introduce world religions to their schools, professional reticence may in fact discourage many of them from the attempt. Less than 40 per cent of the RE teachers in secondary schools have specialist qualifications, and of these only a minority have had world religions courses in colleges or universities. Primary-school teachers are generally responsible for the religious education of their class, but the amount of religious education built into their own initial

*Cf. B. E. Gates, 'The Politics of Religious Education', in M. Taylor (ed.), *Progress and Problems in Moral Education* (Slough, National Foundation for Educational Research, 1975).

**Academic pressure to change this legal requirement has accumulated to such an extent that its death knell has been sounded: J. M. Hull, *School Worship, an Obituary* (London, SCM Press, 1975). Public outcry at the publication of the book indicates the likelihood of delay in the funeral arrangements.

***Religious Education in Primary Schools, Schools Council Working Paper 44 (London, Evans-Methuen, 1972), pp. 27-8 and appendix C.

training as teachers has only exceptionally included world religions.*

The competence and motivation of those who have sought to introduce world religions in their schools is not always above reproach. It is not unknown for a teacher to set about teaching world religions with no more background understanding than that acquired from an introductory school text intended for 12-15-year-olds. The risk of superficiality and distortion is enormous anyway—even for the specialist—but, in such instances as this, 'good intentions' are almost bound to be counter-productive. Unfortunately, publishers sensing the commercial possibilities of an expanding world religions market have sometimes been so eager to join in that they have failed to realise the shoddiness of what they were offering.

As for wrong motivation, there are instances where teachers have made references to different religious traditions only then to go on and compare them unfavourably with the true religion—Christianity. Rather differently, others have come into world religions 'on the rebound' from personal engagement with 'religionless Christianity' and 'death of God' theologies; here the risk may be a naïve exaltation of any faith other than the one in which they have ceased themselves to believe.

The 'world religions revolution', therefore, may be begun but can hardly be described as complete. The enormity of the task, together with counter-revolutionary elements, could threaten the whole movement. Much depends on efforts presently being made within the religious communities and professional academic centres and associations to consolidate the changes already achieved.

PARENT RELIGIOUS COMMUNITIES

The provision for religious education has traditionally been by agreement between churches and local education authorities. The Agreed Syllabuses from the 1920s to the late 1960s were successive local attempts to arrive at a common-denominator version of Christianity which could unobjectionably be taught in a public educational system. However diverse the range of belief and unbelief in English society during this period, the Christian community was institutionally established as the nation's norm.

Thus, the Jewish community, settled in the country for over 300 years, now numbering 400,000 to 500,000, and no longer confined to

*On the limitations of the present staffing of religious education in schools, cf. H. Marratt, *Recruitment, Employment and Training of Teachers of Religious Education* (London, British Council of Churches, 1971); 'The Lancashire Religious Education Survey', in *Learning for Living*, Vol. 14, no. 5, May 1975, pp. 170-86, 193.

two or three ghetto areas, could yet be effectively ignored by the syllabus-makers. Indeed, the Old Testament treated only as a prolego-menon to the Christian tradition, and Pharisaic piety presented in imprisoning contrast to the gospel of liberation added insult to the injury of nigh-total silence about the Jewish story beyond 70 CE.

Neither was there much recognition of the position of the unchurched majority of the population.* To be sure, there is negative acknowledgement of the possibility of conscientious objection to Christian-based teaching in schools, in the withdrawal rights guaranteed to pupils' parents by Act of Parliament.** But there was no deliberate representation of non-theistic philosophies of life. This is not made any easier by the fact that only a small proportion of the 'unchurched' are avowed secularists, Marxists or members of the British Humanist Association,*** but with or without such institu-tional labelling their respective allegiances function in their lives in a fashion comparable with religion.

Ironically, legislation that sought to stem the flow of immigration from the Commonwealth and overseas in 1962 affected the entire situation of minority and majority groups in this country. For many of the folk from India and Pakistan, Cyprus or the West Indies found they could no longer return to their homelands without loss of right to re-entry. Thus, migrants became settlers; wives and families were nurtured over here, and the schools by the late 1960s received increasing numbers of children of different complexions, and of which religion was a major distinguishing feature.****

The religious pluralism of English society became so obvious that, in certain areas at least, Christian allegiance was revealed as one amongst many. A local authority conference of Bradford teachers in consultation with minority groups produced a supplement to the West Riding Agreed Syllabus entitled *Guide to Religious Education in a Multi-Faith Community* (1973), in which Christianity was set as equal alongside Hinduism, Islam, Judaism and Sikhism.***** This, and the

*The extent of 'secularisation' in England is disputed; for contrasting analyses, cf. B. Wilson, *Religion in Secular Society* (London, Watts, 1966), and D. Martin, *A Sociology of English Religion* (London, SCM Press, 1967). On the 'minority' status of the Church of England today, cf. T. Ling, 'Religion in England: Majorities and Minorities', in *New Community*, vol. 2, no. 2, Spring 1973, pp. 117-24.

**Guaranteed since the beginning of state education in England; cf. M. Cruickshank, *Church and State in English Education* (London, Macmillan, 1963), ch. 2.

***Cf. C. Campbell, 'Humanism in Britain: the Formation of a Secular Value-Oriented Movement', in D. Martin (ed.), *A Sociological Yearbook of Religion in Britain* (London, SCM Press, 1969).

****I. Morrish, *The Background of Immigrant Children* (London, Allen & Unwin, 1973); E. Krausz, *Ethnic Minorities in Britain* (London, MacGibbon & Kee, 1971).

*****Produced by the YCRC (Yorkshire Committee for Community Relations), W. Owen Cole (ed.), *Religion in the Multi-Faith School: A Tool for Teachers*, 1973.

even more inclusive Birmingham Syllabus, indicates the potential support available from the parent religious communities, including the British Humanist Association, for a broadly based religious education.

Risk to this potential is considerable, both from the professional limitations already mentioned and from inter-faith suspicions. Of particular importance, therefore, are two national bodies that have been established in the last three years.

The first is the Standing Conference on Inter-Faith Dialogue in Education.* It provides a forum in which the communities of faith can informally discuss any matters of common educational concern. At a recent gathering (1975), which was devoted to the process of initiation in education and religion, the following recommendations were agreed:

(1) *County schools and local authorities* to recognise fully the needs (including factors affecting diet, dress and festivals) for all minority communities, and to provide opportunities for them to make their unique contribution to the religious and cultural life of the school.

(2) *Minority communities* to make known their felt needs and aspirations to schools and local authorities, and to encourage their own people to be trained as teachers so that they may play their full part in the county school and in the production of suitable material concerning their own faith for teachers of RE in the county schools.

(3) *Parents and families* of all communities to examine (and perhaps to redefine) their own situation in a pluralist society, to encourage their children who are students in schools and colleges to contribute to the exchange of views with their peers in the fields of morality and religion, and to support the school as well as their own children by participating in its extra-curricular life.

(4) *Support for religious education* conceived 'as a developmental process by which every child, wherever he lives, will have the opportunity of learning about the ideals and insights, religious and non-religious, which inspire mankind' (1974 Inter-Faith Conference Statement) in the belief that religious education so conceived would provide a climate congenial for the participation of all communities.

(5) *Members of Parliament, the Department of Education and Science, local education authorities and the Community*

*Chairman Rabbi Hugo Gryn; Hon. Sec. John Prickett, Little Brunger, Appledore Road, Tenterden, Kent.

Relations Commission and its local council to take note of the above recommendations and to seek ways of implementing them.

Translations were made for publication in the several ethnic newspapers.

The second is the National Religious Education Council.* Like the Standing Conference this includes representatives from every major religious community in the country, along with the British Humanist Association, but all professional organisations (school-, college- and university-oriented) associated with religious education are also officially involved. Representation is formally agreed and the constitution carefully balanced for professional and confessional interests. Where once the Government's Ministry of Education primarily consulted the churches about matters pertaining to religious education, this council is now the most authoritative advisory body, and tacitly recognised as such.

Parent religious communities, therefore, are making a significant contribution to the cause of teaching of world religions. There is a domestic consequence for them, however. In addition to provision for study of their own faith, they are faced with an urgent theological priority—that of coming to terms with the plurality of religious truth claims. The logic of the Christian faith, for instance, requires that some positive sense be made of this world and of all that is in it, including other religions.** A Christian education would in itself be incomplete without direct dealing with the faith of other folk.*** This is true of the other communities too. Thus the mutual involvement of schools and communities, which is an important feature of the English scene, has in this way become a spur to theological explorations. In turn, any one tradition drawing on its own theology of education may throw up questions about prevalent educational assumptions.****

---

*Chairman Edwin Cox, Senior Lecturer in Religious Education, University of London Institute of Education, Malet Street, London.

**Cf. W. E. Hocking, *Living Religions and a World Faith* (New York, Macmillan, 1940); P. Tillich, *Christianity and the Encounter of the World Religions* (New York, Columbia University Press, 1963) and *The Future of Religions* (New York, Harper & Row, 1966); W. A. Christian, *Oppositions of Religious Doctrines* (London, Macmillan, 1972); J. Hick (ed.), *Truth and Dialogue: the Relationship between World Religions* (London, Sheldon Press, 1974).

***N. Smart, *Secular Education and the Logic of Religion* (London, Faber, 1968); Durham Report, *The Fourth R* (London, SPCK, 1970), pp. 61-3, 102-3.

****Cf. N. Ferré, *Theology for Christian Education* (Philadelphia, Westminster, 1967); 'Towards a Hindu Theory of Creativity', *Education Theory*, vol. 20, no. 4, Fall 1970, pp. 368-75; H. S. Broudy, 'Sartre's Existentialism and Education', in *Education Theory*, vol. 21, no. 2, Spring 1971, pp. 155-77; A. L. Tibawi, *Muslim Education: Its Tradition and Modernisation* (London, Luzac, 1972).

PROFESSIONAL ACADEMIC CONCERNS

The long-term strength of the movement towards teaching world religions needs also to be guaranteed by professional academic developments. The revolution was philosophically propelled, almost independently of the recognition of religious pluralism in the country. A professional consensus emerged that religion's place in any curriculum had to be justified 'on educational grounds', and seen to be so.*

The consensus in part reflected the concern with the philosophy of education that burgeoned in the mid-1960s. Curriculum philosophers focused attention on the different forms of knowledge, and thus questions about the logical status and distinctiveness of religion were raised. The more abrasive took the priority given to the Bible throughout English education as indication of covert assumptions about special revelation, predicated on faith rather than on reason. The school of reason should not be confused with any stable of revelation! Others recognised an alternative perspective in the philosophy of religion.

For, simultaneously with these concerns in the philosophy of education, the pattern for the study of religion in universities was changing. Theology, however scientifically studied, had in university usage meant predominantly the Old and New Testaments, church history and doctrine. The now generally accepted change of nomenclature to departments of religious studies which has taken place since 1966 (when the first was established at the University of Lancaster) represents an acknowledgement that these elements form part of the larger Christian tradition, which in turn is part of the larger religious experience of mankind. University theological horizons are expected to be comprehensive;** even as a result of historical accident the study of religion in a public educational system should not remain sectarian. Acceptance of this point provides the second ingredient of the professional consensus.

These academic concerns are effectively conjoined with those of the parent religious communities on the National Religious Education

*J. M. Hull, 'Religious Education in a Pluralist Society' in M. Taylor (ed.), *Progress and Problems in Moral Education*; B. E. Gates, 'Religious Education: a Proper Humanism', in *London Educational Review*, vol. 2, no. 3, Autumn 1973, pp. 55-61; *Religious Education in Secondary Schools*, Schools Council Working Paper 36 (London, Evans/Methuen, 1971).

**N. Smart, 'Religion as a Subject', in *Church Quarterly Review,* vol. 2, no. 3, January 1970, pp. 227-33; A. D. Galloway, 'Theology and Religious Studies—the Unity of Our Discipline', in *Religious Studies*, vol. 11, no. 2, June 1975, pp. 157-66; E. G. Parrinder, 'Religious Studies in Great Britain', in *Religion* (IAHR 13th Congress Issue), August 1975, pp. 1-11.

Council. Immediately, criteria are operative in the selection of priorities for religious education which are not dependent on the present composition of English society and local variations. Otherwise, the fact that there are as many followers of the Bahai faith in England as there are Buddhists might be made to justify giving these two traditions equal weight. Or, again, distinctive dress and numerical strength of the Sikh community might be a distraction from the claims for due attention of the Hindu tradition, slightly smaller in its English representation. Similarly, the relative absence of immigrants from such parts of the country as Cornwall or Hereford or Cumbria might be presented as a reason for ignoring there any faith other than Christianity. Against these kinds of danger, the disciplines of religious studies and the larger context of the religious experience of mankind provide a necessary guard. The task of selection from within such inclusive horizons remains daunting, however, and definitional disputes among scholars compound the difficulty.* The most systematic attempt to deal with this question of criteria in religious education has been by a group of philosophers and educationists appointed by the Schools Council to produce a taxonomy of religious education. Their 'groundplan' for the subject, with its selection of salient concepts, skills and attitudes from respective religious traditions, is greatly needed.**

This Schools Council report should serve as further theoretical consolidation for the revolution. But arguably the most urgent consolidation is with teacher education. In this field much pioneering has been done by the Shap Working Party on World Religions in Education. Established in 1969, and consisting of teachers and lecturers from all levels of education, it sponsors regular in-service courses all over the country on world religions. The courses have been designed to give intensive introductions to a particular religious tradition and to give guidance about classroom application. Response in Wales and Northern Ireland has been limited, less so in Scotland, but in England their success has been such that many local education authorities and teachers' centres are now offering similar courses. In

---

*Cf. W. C. Smith, *The Meaning and End of Religion* (New York, Macmillan, 1962); M. E. Spiro, 'Religion: Problems of Definition and Explanation', in M. Banton (ed.), *Anthropological Approaches to the Study of Religion* (London, Tavistock Publications, 1966), pp. 85-126; R. D. Baird, *Category Formation in the History of Religions* (The Hague, Mouton, 1971); N. Smart, *The Phenomenon of Religion* (London, Macmillan, 1973) and *The Science of Religion and the Sociology of Knowledge: Some Methodological Questions* (Princeton University Press, 1973); F. J. Strong, *Ways of Being Religious* (Prentice-Hall, 1973).

**In making its selections the working party sought assistance and comment from the religious communities themselves, via the National Religious Education Council.

addition to the courses, the Shap Working Party provides a general information service on world religions, and has a series of regionally based working groups, which concentrate on such priorities as world religions in the infant school and in public examinations.* Independently, the two national resource centres for religious education, government-financed, and a similar Church of England centre carry most of the available world religions 'teaching aids', and actively encourage this approach to the subject.**

Such provisions for in-service re-education, together with those presently being trained in universities and colleges, may eventually mean that the world religions revolution is practically as well as theoretically reinforced.

THE HERMENEUTICS OF TEACHING

During the transition period, and probably beyond, there are likely to be different ways of teaching world religions. In history teaching, there is continuing dispute as to whether it is more effective to take a 'grand survey' approach or to concentrate on a much more specific time and place. Is it misleading to build a year's work around a few key figures? Would it be more instructive to focus on social and economic conditions? Is it possible to single out some central concern which can be said to be the prime objective of history teaching—for example, 'sense of time perspective'—and to work consistently for that?*** Comparable questions are asked about teaching world religions, with no immediate prospect of final solution.

The ambiguity of suggesting that a *historical approach* should be employed is already clear. But psychological considerations further complicate the matter. Some who have taken the historical tack have ignored the findings of developmental psychology about children's capacities for chronological understanding.**** Others sadly report the

---

*Secretary John Rankin, Head of Religious Studies, Bishop Otter College, Chichester. Publications include P. Woodward (ed.), *World Religions: Aids for Teachers*, 2nd edn. (London, Community Relations Commission, 1973); E. J. Sharpe and J. R. Hinnells, *Hinduism*. The Shap Working Party now publishes an annual mailing; for details please write to the secretary enclosing an s.a.e.

**D. Brennan, Religious Education Centre, Borough Road College, Isleworth, Middlesex; M. Grimmitt, Religious Education Centre, Westhill College, Birmingham. The Church's centre is at St Gabriel's College, Cormont Road, London. It has a satellite at the College of Ripon and York, St John's, Lord Mayor's Walk, York.

***Cf. W. H. Burston and C. W. Green, *Handbook for History Teachers*, 2nd edn. (London, Methuen, 1972).

****Psychological findings reviewed by A. Godin, 'Some Developmental Tasks in Christian Education', in M. Strommen (ed.), *Research on Religious Development* (New York, Hawthorn, 1971), pp. 109-54.

disinterest of their pupils when faced with the Indus Valley civilisation —a response previously familiar in dealing with the history and archaeology of Israel.

A *phenomenological approach* has appeared to some to provide a more effective alternative. But in school versions this has sometimes meant little more than visits (audio-visually arranged, if local resources were otherwise limited) to temples and synagogues, and tales of 'founders' and festivals. By these means, familiarity with external trappings may have been achieved, but not necessarily appreciation of what it means to be a Sikh or a Jew.

A more personal emphasis has been present in an *archetypal approach*. Especially in the primary school, this has involved the selection of certain themes, such as trust, light, wonder, helping, representing basic elements in religion. Personal engagement may have been created as a result, but often variations between religions have been blurred. Common denominators of what it means to be religious are not so easily available, and the Humanists in particular are wary of the 'conversion by definition' which they fear might follow from presenting everyday human concerns as religious.

To a certain extent, assessment of the limitations and relative merits of such different ways of teaching world religions depends upon the resolution of methodological issues in the academic study of religion. An educationally balanced procedure will probably include each of the main emphases here represented as separate approaches. As in the historical approach, there will be the priority of factual detail and perspective; as in the phenomenological, the priority of structures of meaning and distanced understanding; and, as in the archetypal, that of locating common human concerns. But a major responsibility must lie with individual teachers. They have a double loyalty—to the religious experience of mankind in all its diversity, and to the individual experience of children. This entails hermeneutical skills in both directions at once.

The child-centredness characteristic of primary-school education, if consistently applied to the teaching of world religions, can be a guard against 'inert' learning. But, more important, it can also mean that teachers are sensitive to the range of individual understandings in any group of children. A teacher is their interpreter.

At the same time, teachers must have interpreted and understood at their own level the aspects of religion which they wish to share with the children. Such sensitive hermeneutics should prevent superficiality or syncretistic distortion. Thus, by this double commitment to the children in their own right and religion in its own terms, the dialectic of reason and revelation in religious understanding can itself be respected.

Something of this dialectic may have been lost in too simplistic applications of Ninian Smart's six-dimensional model of religion to religious education (see Table 1). So widely has this been disseminated through the Schools Council Projects on Religious Education and other literature* that in the space of five years it has become for some, as it were, a new Hexateuch. This typology of the major constituent elements of religion—doctrinal, mythical, ritual, ethical, social, experiential**—has served to highlight the multi-dimensional character of religion, an invaluable reminder in a situation where even 'Christian man' was cast in syllabus terms as 'one-dimensional'. The danger is real, however, that the dynamic intent of the scheme, essentially dependent on the distinctive expressions of any one tradition of faith, may be obscured. Religion may once again be conveniently packaged—and lifeless.

This risk will be all the greater unless the correspondence between the components of being religious and those of being human is appreciated. For each religious component is reflective of elemental aspects of human being, as can be illustrated most easily by the accompanying chart. In seeking to further a child's religious understanding, their general/secular understanding is also inevitably involved.

Table 1   *'Secular' counterparts to Smart's constituent elements of being 'religious'*

'Secular'	*'Religious'*
formal reasoning in science, mathematics, or history	Doctrine
story-telling and gossip	Myth
ordering of personal interests, priorities, ambitions	Ethics
playground games and gestures of friendship	Ritual
intimate feelings of self-awareness	Experience
social and political belonging, in family and school	Social

The objective of a religious education defined in such terms would not necessarily be to make a child 'religious'. The logic of a plural religious situation in society entails recognition that there are many different ways of being religious and irreligious, and in a public system

*Ninian Smart, Professor of Religious Studies at the University of Lancaster, has been Director of two of the Schools Council Projects on Religious Education, the Secondary one 1969-72, and the Primary one 1973-6. His most recent writing on religious education is 'The Exploration of Religion and Education', in *Oxford Review of Education*, vol. 1, no. 2, 1975, pp. 99-105. The model has become the basis for the Projects' own approach and publications, and that of others, e.g. M. Grimmitt, *What Can I Do in Religious Education?* (Great Wakering, Mayhew-McCrimmon, 1973); S. Kronenburg and P. Longley, *Discovering Religion Workcards* (Guildford, Lutterworth Educational, 1972).

**Developed in *Secular Education and the Logic of Religion*, pp. 15-18 and *Religious Experience of Mankind* (New York, Scribners, 1969), pp. 6-12.

of education the truth claims of none can be taken for granted at the expense of the others. It would be entirely proper, by contrast, for a school to seek to enable a child to become 'religiate'; in other words, to enable him to understand what it might mean to be religious—in, for example, Catholic or Protestant, Buddhist or Muslim terms—or what it might mean to reject religion in the name of Marx, or Freud, or Sartre.

Understanding of this kind would complement any personal religious identity or questing, bequeathed by the home or parent religious community. By providing the human checkpoints for different religious and atheistic viewpoints, it would challenge blinkered attitudes and encourage careful pondering about their respective beliefs and values, both as separate symbolic constellations and as impinging on each other.

TEACHING WORLD RELIGIONS: RELIGIOUS EDUCATION

In the 'early days' of the movement towards teaching world religions, the possibility was discussed of treating them separately from (Christian) religious education.* This would have preserved the traditional provision of induction into the Christian tradition while allowing world religions to be taught in a manner free from any evangelistic aims. But, as well as proving unrealistic in terms of the overcrowded school-timetable, its division of labour was too simple. As already indicated, Christian education in itself requires reference to the faith of other folk and their alternative claims to truth; openness in this regard can be a model for educators in any religious community. Moreover, it is a mistake to suppose that it were educational to ignore the vitality of other faiths.

Instead, therefore, of speaking about 'teaching world religions' the term 'RE' itself can now fairly be used to include this orientation. The time for artificial polarisation between Bible teaching and life-concerns, between teaching Christianity or teaching world religions, is passing. An authentic religious education for the future involves wholehearted initiation into the manifold structures of religious experience of mankind and the rich diversity of human being.**

*So J. R. Hinnells, 'The Comparative Study of Religion in West Riding Schools', in *Comparative Religion in Education* (London, Oriel/Routledge, 1970).

**In addition to books already mentioned, one which combines a world religious orientation with Christian theological concern and practical classroom experience is J. Holm, *Teaching Religion in School* (Oxford University Press, 1975).

Booklist

W. O. Cole (ed.), *Religion in the Multi-Faith School* (Yorkshire Committee for Community Relations, Charlton House, Hunslet Road, Leeds, 1973).

W. O. Cole (ed.), *World Religions: a Handbook for Teachers* (Commission for Racial Equality, 2nd edn, 1977).

J. Finel (ed.), *World Religions for CSE or 16 Plus* (SWP, Brunner School, Billingham, Cleveland, 1975).

J. R. Hinnells (ed.), *Comparative Religion in Education* (Oriel Press, 1970).

J. R. Hinnells and E. J. Sharpe (eds), *Hinduism* (Oriel Press, 1972).

Jean Holm, *Teaching Religion in School* (Oxford University Press, 1975).

Religious Education in Secondary Schools, Schools Council Working Paper 36 (Evans/Methuen, 1971).

N. Smart and D. Horder (eds), *New Movements in Religious Education* (Temple Smith, 1975).

Discovering an Approach, Schools Council (Macmillan Education, 1977).

Index